BISL®
POCKET GUIDE

Other publications by Van Haren Publishing

Van Haren Publishing (VHP) specializes in titles on Best Practices, methods and standards within four domains:
- IT and IT Management
- Architecture (Enterprise and IT)
- Business management and
- Project management

Van Haren Publishing offers a wide collection of whitepapers, templates, free e-books, trainer material etc. in the **Van Haren Publishing Knowledge Base**: www.vanharen.net for more details.

Van Haren Publishing is also publishing on behalf of leading organizations and companies: ASLBiSL Foundation, CA, Centre Henri Tudor, Gaming Works, IACCM, IAOP, IPMA-NL, ITSqc, NAF, Ngi, PMI-NL, PON, The Open Group, The SOX Institute.

Topics are (per domain):

IT and IT Management	Architecture (Enterprise and IT)	Project Management
ABC of ICT	Archimate®	A4-Projectmanagement
ASL®	BIP / Novius	ICB / NCB
CATS CM®	GEA®	MINCE®
CMMI®	TOGAF®	M_o_R®
CoBIT		MSP™
Frameworx	**Business Management**	P3O®
ISO 17799	BiSL®	*PMBOK® Guide*
ISO 27001	Contract Management	PRINCE2®
ISO 27002	EFQM	
ISO/IEC 20000	eSCM	
ISPL	ISA-95	
IT Service CMM	ISO 9000	
ITIL®	ISO 9001:2000	
MOF	OPBOK	
MSF	SAP	
SABSA	SixSigma	
	SOX	
	SqEME®	

BiSL®

POCKET GUIDE

Remko van der Pols
Yvette Backer

Van Haren
PUBLISHING

Colophon

Title:	BiSL® – Pocket Guide
Authors:	Remko van der Pols
	Yvette Backer
Editor of the English translation:	Steve Newton
Reviewers of the Dutch first edition:	Richard de Beer, IVENT, Ministerie van Defensie
	Glenn Coert, Ordina Infrastructure Solutions
	Rick Dekker, Gyata BPI Consultants
	Jeroen Eijskoot, VTS Politie Nederland
	Bert Franken, Bbusi BV
	Harrie Kisters, Gartner
Publisher:	Van Haren Publishing www.vanharen.net
ISBN:	Hard copy 978 90 8753 711 1
	eBook 978 80 8753 812 5
Print:	Second edition, first impression, September 2012
Layout and design:	CO2 Premedia, Amersfoort - NL
Cover design:	CO2 Premedia, Amersfoort - NL
Copyright:	2012 ASL BiSL Foundation/Van Haren Publishing

For any further enquiries about Van Haren Publishing, please send an e-mail to:
info@vanharen.net

Foreword

Effective management of business information is critically important for today's organizations, covering all the activities for controlling information provisioning. This is the domain in which managers of business information, system owners, product managers, information managers and Chief Information officers (CIOs) operate.

This Pocket Guide describes BiSL, Business information Services Library, a framework for business information management and information management. BiSL is a public domain standard that is consistent with ITIL® and ASL® (Application Services Library).

The information in this Pocket Guide helps managers to adopt a professional approach to the management of their business information. It draws on the practical experiences of organizations that are using this framework and builds on the lessons learned from those experiences. It provides a description of the framework, together with a detailed definition of a standard for business information management.

Remko van der Pols,
Yvette Backer

Contents

1 Business information management and BiSL

1.1 Introduction

The book *BiSL, a framework for business information management* produced the first public domain standard for business information management available to everyone. BiSL, Business information Services Library, describes the processes of business information management and, supported through the use of best practices and aids, completes and improves these processes. This *Pocket Guide* describes this process model in an accessible manner.[1]

1.2 What is business information management?

Organizations carry out business processes and various production means are used. Examples of these include:

- Organization and the managing body
- Money and other financial means
- Personnel
- Buildings and other types of property
- Machines
- Information provisioning.

---

1 A note regarding the terminology used. There are many various ideas as to what business information management is. We shall therefore be dealing with this in detail in this chapter and describe the domain of business information management. One of the conclusions will be that business information management includes both operational and strategic processes and activities.

Business information management deals with the final of these
production factors: namely information provisioning. Contrary
to widespread belief, information provisioning is considerably
more than just IT (information- and communication technology).
IT is the entire technical means used to carry out information
provisioning. IT is a realization and an implementation of *a
part of* the information provisioning. Information provisioning
deals with the information used to carry out and manage the
business process and to manage the organization. For this, IT
is often used, as are procedures, work instructions and manual
administration; people are also a part of this.

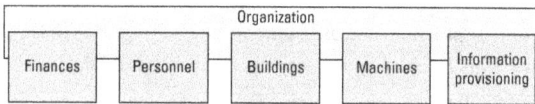

Figure 1 The production means within an organization

Business information management is the part of an organization
that deals with the management of information provisioning,
its design and adaptation, and maintaining and monitoring the
working of information provisioning. This is not a question of
technology but logic and its logical use.

Types of *IT management*
Business information management therefore monitors the
business approach to information provisioning. In most
organizations this information provisioning also has an IT
component that relates to the technical means used to deliver
this. These means are managed and developed by another type
of organization, the IT function. There are a few different types
of management within the IT function. There is commonly

a division that distinguishes between the so-called IT infrastructure management and application management.

IT infrastructure management provides and manages the technical infrastructure. These are the physical means, typically including standardized facilities, on which information provisioning operates. This therefore deals with servers, PC's, networks, printers, operating systems (such as MS Windows) and standard software such as browsers, word processors etc. Here, people fulfil positions such as network- and system administrator. Application management deals with the maintenance, use and renewal of applications including business packages such as SAP, Oracle and Exact. Here, people fulfill positions such as (functional or technical) designer, data analyst, programmer and tester.

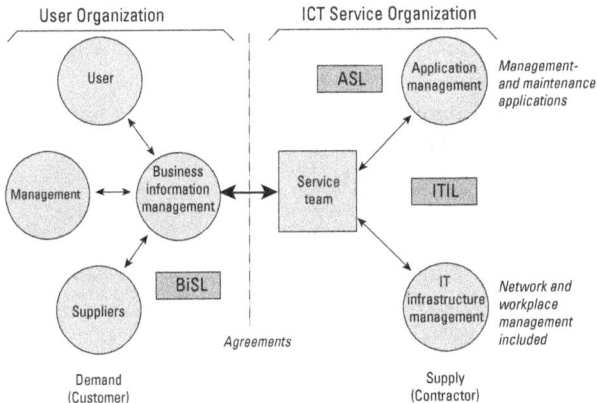

Figure 2 Process standards for management and relations between these

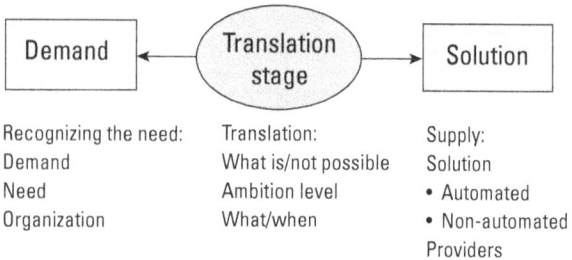

Demand	Translation stage	Solution

Recognizing the need: Translation: Supply:
Demand   What is/not possible   Solution
Need   Ambition level   • Automated
Organization   What/when   • Non-automated
                                                   Providers

Figure 3 The translation stage between demand and supply

Two standards are of importance for the process organization
of the management and organization of the services within IT
functions: ITIL® and ASL®. Figure 2 shows the domains and the
areas of influence of BiSL, ASL and ITIL.

The position of business information management
Business information management is part of the user
organization. There are of course exceptions to this rule: it is
sometimes executed by the internal IT department. Business
information management is a function that deals with:
• Supporting the use of information provisioning.
• Mapping out the needs for information provisioning or
  changes in this.
• Translating and formulating these needs into a concrete
  demand for IT support (i.e., the solution from the user's
  perspective) and non-automated information provisioning.
• Deciding what is and what is not to be done, when it is to be
  done and the level to which it will be carried out.
• Determining and drafting the long-term perspectives of
  information provisioning.

Business information management does not require expert knowledge of IT. One could say that business information management understands the business processes and this is combined with a feeling for and understanding of IT and the control of IT. Business information management can also be considered a widely qualified purchasing function of the information provisioning, acting as the principal for IT organizations.

As mentioned earlier, information provisioning includes more than just an automated part. Non-automated information provisioning (whether or not formal) is at least as important. This is formed by procedures, work instructions, and regulations on how to use information systems, together with manual or semi-automated administration such as spreadsheets and card-index boxes.

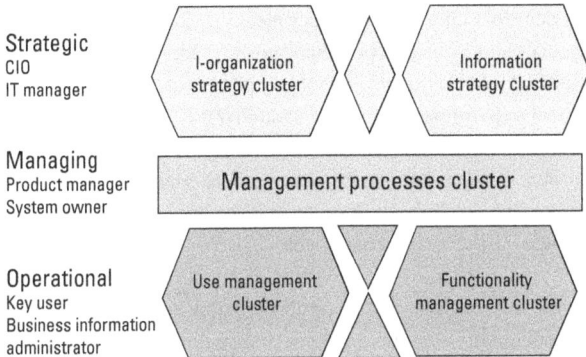

Strategic
CIO
IT manager

I-organization strategy cluster

Information strategy cluster

Managing
Product manager
System owner

Management processes cluster

Operational
Key user
Business information administrator

Use management cluster

Functionality management cluster

Figure 4 The three levels of control of business information management

Relationship between business information administration and information management

Business information management is a function, an organization that manages the information provisioning and its use. There are three levels within business information management:

- The operational level– on this level, the use and the intrinsic design of information provisioning are managed. Here, the content and the completion of information provisioning are of central importance. This is called business information administration (in some publications functional management).
- The managing level– this involves the management of such things as time, quality, money, agreements and contracts.
- The strategic level – on this level, information provisioning and its organization and management are designed on a more long-term basis. This is often called information management.

It is clear that information management (which in many organizations is the function that deals with formulating policy regarding information provisioning) operates in the same domain as business information administration. It can be said that information management is the strategic level of business information management. Equally, it can also be said that business information administration is the operational level of business information management.

For the sake of clarity of the argument in this Pocket Guide, we shall use the coordinating term 'Business information management' to indicate the entire domain. This therefore also covers the activities often indicated by the terms 'information management' or 'business information administration'.

The field of influence in which business information management operates

It can be seen from the above that business information management is important for the successful organization and operation of the business processes. Business information management must try to achieve the optimum between possibilities and impossibilities, offering the following four perspectives:

- This involves a business process and users in which information provisioning plays an important and often essential role. Businesses processes change sometimes and information provisioning must change with it. However, users cannot change as often or as fast, since it is normally not so easy to change one's way of working and the business process must continue during the change.
- Also in the control of IT and IT providers, business information management is often confronted with limitations. For example, an average organization has no control over Microsoft with regards to the functionality of its word processor.
- Business information management also deals with finite possibilities, capacities and qualities from one's own business information management organization.
- Finally, one acts within the policy and frameworks of organization, or within the frameworks that dictate external factors such as legislation and chain management. The frameworks are the starting point for business processes and business information management. However, business information management also realizes this policy: the information policy is made by business information management and the possibilities and impossibilities of information provisioning also have an influence on the policy of the organization.

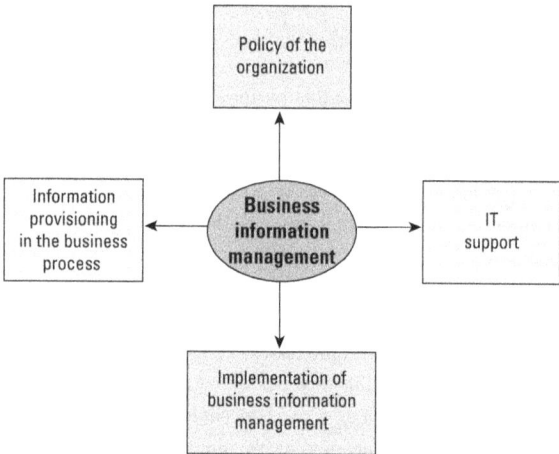

Figure 5 The field of influence within which business information management must operate

The organization of business information management
Seldom is business information management or the control of business information management to be found in one place within an organization. There are often several business information management functions or business information management is controlled from several places. This may seem undesirable but it is often logical and inevitable in many organizations.

In most organizations, the finance manager or finance director is responsible for the financial information provisioning of the organization. Similarly, the personnel manager or personnel director is responsible for the personnel information provisioning, the marketing director is responsible for an organization's services to major clients, and the director of private sectors is responsible for the private market. For all these directors, information provisioning is essential for the day-to-day operation of the organization. For this reason, they wish to be able to control information provisioning directly, which means that they control business information management directly, or aspire to do so.

This is why an organization often has several information domains with the associated Business information management.

In the example shown in Figure 6, there are five business information management (BIM) groups. There is a group that deals with the logistical information provisioning, one that deals with personnel information provisioning and one for the financial information provisioning.

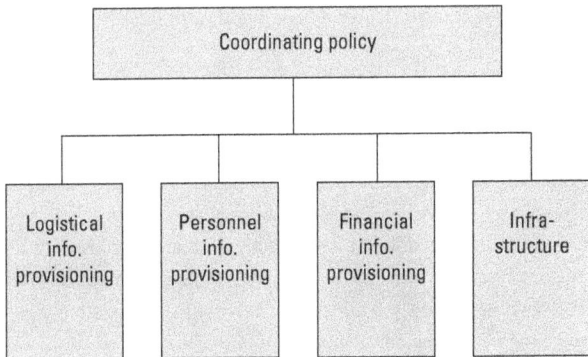

Figure 6 Example of an architecture with information domains

There is also, as in many organizations, a slightly different group for technical infrastructure; this includes work places and the standard infrastructure of the organization. There is also a corporate group, which deals with the overall policy of the organization in the area of information provisioning.

The method and the extent to which the business information management takes place and the way in which information provisioning is managed depends on the form of authority in the organization. An important factor for the successful operation of business information management is the extent to which the lines of powers that it incorporates follow those that are already in place within the user organization.

The consequence is that there is seldom one point from which information provisioning of an organization is managed. Who carries out the management and how it is managed must therefore be clearly agreed. BiSL deals separately with this.

1.3   Objectives of BiSL

As a result of the professionalization of the IT services in past years, there has been an increasing imbalance as the demand organization, business information management, has been left behind and has thus become the weak link. Also, from a business perspective, the need for a more effective and more efficient use of information provisioning and better end user support has grown significantly. This means that many organizations are giving increasing consideration to business information management. And here's where BiSL comes up in discussion. The ASL BiSL Foundation sets BiSL the following objectives:

• Offering recognition of the important activities that people carry out within the organization in the area of business information management and giving consideration with regards to the importance of this.

- Positioning business information management in its environment and ensuring this fits in well with other process models such as ASL and ITIL.
- Offering one language and a joint jointly supported framework for the completion and carrying out of business information management.
- Offering tangible support in the carrying out and ongoing improvement of business information management such as the provisioning of best practices.
- Offering clarity, completeness and coherence in the areas of procurement, design and the use of information provisioning, as well as recognizing that business information management operates in the same domain.
- Re-using knowledge in this regard and offering a platform for information exchange.

1.4   Promotion by way of a foundation

BiSL is a *public domain* standard, which means that the body of thought is within an independent foundation making it freely available to everyone. This is the ASL BiSL Foundation, a foundation that also manages Application Services Library, ASL.

With the introduction of BiSL and the transfer of BiSL to the ASL BiSL Foundation, the objectives of the ASL BiSL Foundation have been widened. The decision to include BiSL in this foundation offers various advantages:

- It is now possible to make use of the existing facilities and best practices from such a foundation.
- It can be guaranteed that BiSL and ASL fit together and will continue to do so.

More information on this is available on www.aslbislfoundation.
org, see also Annex 3.

1.5   Objectives and structure of this booklet

The objective of this Pocket Guide is not to teach someone how
to organize business information management and information
management, or exactly how BiSL is organized and what
activities take place. It is an introduction, whereby we want to
illustrate to the reader the importance, extent and coherence
of the activities within the domain of business information
management. It is also an introduction to BiSL that provides
an insight into the structure, set-up and global interpretation of
BiSL in an business accessible a manner as possible. The reader
will also get a feel for the processes, the importance of organizing
these properly and the circumstances that can potentially cause
problems. For business information managers, information
managers and business information administrators, this Pocket
Guide is hopefully a world of recognition; for outsiders and
managers, it is an easy means of gaining a better view of this area.

This first chapter dealt with setting out the domain of business
information management, the basic considerations, and what the
content and key values are. The next chapter deals with the set-up
of BiSL. The following chapters then address the process clusters
of BiSL. The processes and activities in the various clusters are
illustrated using a case study that is followed throughout the book.
The last chapter briefly describes how to start working with BiSL.

Background to the case study is included in Annex 1 and should
be read before working through the various chapters that contain
references to the case study – otherwise it can be quite difficult to
follow.

2 The BiSL framework

2.1 Introduction

The BiSL framework consists of various processes grouped together in clusters. The processes in these clusters are closely connected and are similar in many ways to the nature of management, incorporating the necessary knowledge and experience of the employees in the business information management organization.

BiSL has process clusters on the strategic, managing and operational levels, see also Figure 7. The complete diagram of BiSL is included in Annex 5.

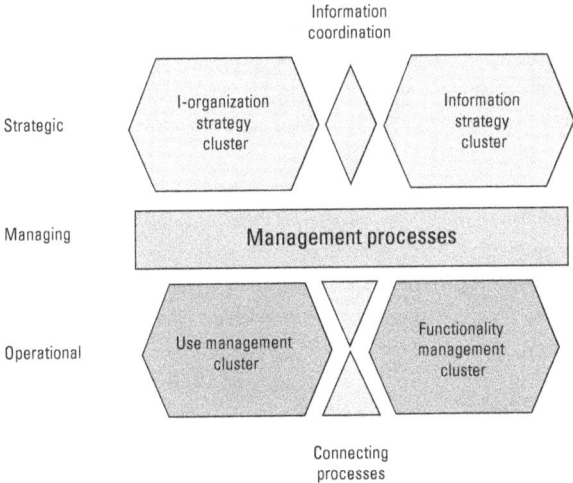

Figure 7 The BiSL framework

2.2   The operational processes

There are three process clusters on the operational level.

Use management cluster

The central point of the *use management* cluster is to ensure that the existing information provisioning provides optimal support to the business processes and that these are used adequately. Here, the users are supported in the optimal use of information provisioning, the operational data management is guaranteed, and the operational control for the maintenance of information provisioning is carried out by the IT providers.

Functionality management cluster

In the *functionality management* cluster the changes to information provisioning are analyzed, worked out and the organization is prepared for the change. This demands, as in the previous cluster, knowledge of information provisioning, the specific needs, and the method used in the business process.

Connecting processes cluster

This cluster ensures that the correct changes to information provisioning are carried out in practice, so they can then be operated by the users. It therefore provides synchronization between the *use management* and *functionality management* clusters.

2.3   The managing processes

The *management processes* cluster ensures that the means (in the widest sense) are available for information provisioning, and that its use is managed in line with the needs and possibilities of the organization. This involves management resources such as time and capacity, costs and benefits, needs, services of suppliers, and contracts. This leads to the overall management of information provisioning, and the activities in this area are independent from how they are managed within the organization.

2.4   The strategic processes

On the strategic level, there are also three clusters.

Information strategy cluster
The *information strategy* cluster deals with the design of information provisioning in the longer term, recognizing what is necessary to achieve this and outlining scenarios in order to achieve the desired situation. This is also referred to as information policy.

I-organization strategy cluster
The *I-organization strategy* cluster refers to the organization of information provisioning. In this cluster the strategy is determined in terms of the form this organization should take and what the roles and responsibilities of the various divisions are. This policy refers to the role of suppliers, the relations with chain partners, the relations with the user organization, and provides direction to the set-up and method of the entire business information management in the organization.

Connecting strategic processes: information coordination
There are typically several parties who develop policies on various parts of information provisioning and the information provisioning organization. This cluster, which consists of one process of *information coordination,* deals with the coordination and communication of the various forms of policy developed in the previous clusters.

2.5   Relations and coherence between clusters

The activities in the area of business information management –
incorporating the activities within the clusters – are carried
out in most organizations at several and various locations and
sometimes also outside of the organization. It is however the
coherence that makes management of information provisioning
work effectively. Here are a few examples.

Use management looks at the operational shortcomings and the
possibilities for the optimal use of information provisioning,
together with how information provisioning can fit in with the
business processes more efficiently and more effectively.

Functionality management deals with the completion and
design of information provisioning. Shortcomings noted within
use management must be solved correctly. The form that the
functionality takes also has a direct influence on the effectiveness
and efficiency in the way that information provisioning is used.

The *management processes* must ensure that any targets
associated with issues such as money and time are adequately
addressed. For important shortcomings and optimization, the
means of removing these or carrying them out must be identified.
Also, strategic developments must be translated into possibilities,
so that these can be dealt with in *functionality management*.

To ensure that successful policies are developed, the strategic
processes need input that, for example, relate to the quality of
the use and integration of the existing information provisioning
with the business processes. The scenarios outlined within the
strategic processes must be feasible and fit in with users and
business processes.

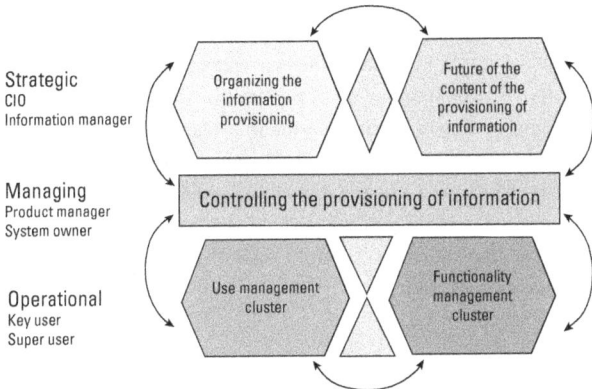

Figure 8 Relationships and connections between the BiSL clusters

There are several more dependencies and information flows than those outlined above. It is not possible to optimally carry out all of the activities in a cluster without information from the other processes. It is therefore important that this information from the various clusters be distributed among the other clusters, so the correct considerations and choices can be made.

This seems trivial but is not. In the majority of organizations this information exchange is less than perfect. Information policy is often formulated without any common ground with the actual situation, the established and future needs. Structural problems with information provisioning such as experienced by users on the shop floor are often not recognized or not understood. An organization will often carry on struggling with the same problems for years, or this policy is not implemented at the management level, so that no specific actions and plans evolve for addressing these.

An important objective of BiSL is understanding that the coherence of activities makes the management and control more effective. The operational processes are the hands and eyes, the managing processes are the steering wheel, and the strategic processes are the map reader and the route. If you don't know where you are, there's no point reading the map. If you wish to go in a certain direction, you have to head that way. You need eyes to see whether you are going in the right direction. It is coherence that makes this effective.

3 Use management cluster

3.1 Introduction

Use management is the first cluster of processes within business information management. *Use management* ensures that the working and the use of information provisioning remain guaranteed and that users are supported in the use of information provisioning.

This cluster is the most critical of all processes. Here, it is ensured that information provisioning works and is used efficiently. This means that the activities in this area underpin all others. However, this does not mean that these activities are always visible for management and that they have been explicitly stated. The historical roots of business information management reside in the *use management* and *functionality management* clusters but nevertheless one has only recently seen consideration for this arise.

In the *use management* cluster, the use and working of information provisioning are of central importance to the organization. There are three aspects of importance in this:

- The users: they must use information provisioning correctly and will sometimes need assistance in this.
- The business information in information provisioning: the central theme of information provisioning. Correctness, completeness and timeliness of data, and provisioning of details on information (such as management information) are the key aspects here.

- The automated information provisioning and the specific control of this.

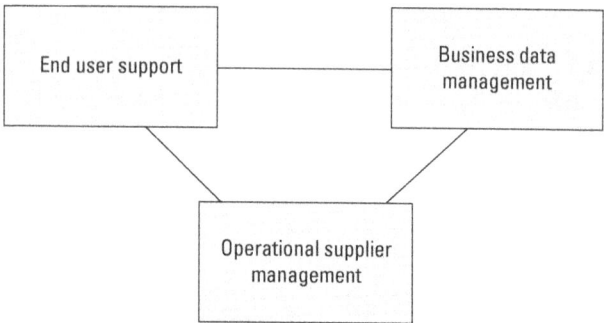

Figure 9 The processes and subjects within the Use management cluster

BiSL therefore recognizes three processes within the *use management* cluster (see also Annex 5):
- *End user support* – the daily contact point for users in the case of questions, complaints or problems.
- *Business data management*– mainly ensures the quality of the data in information provisioning.
- *Operational supplier management* – the (operational) management of automated information provisioning.

3.2   End user support

End user support ensures communication with the end user on the use of the information provisioning. There are two ways in which this communication takes place:
- Users have questions, complaints or needs and business information management deals with these.

- Business information management gives proactive information, for example, on changes in the information provisioning or useful ways of doing things.

Within *end user support,* the business information administrator mainly deals with the handling of questions, wishes, complaints and otherwise, providing the proactive communication on how to use information provisioning, changes in use or availability, etc. *End user support* is very important for business information management: there is daily contact with the end user and it becomes clear how information provisioning is used. This *end user support* can be handled by a separate business information management desk, or as part of the IT service desk, depending on the situation within an organization.

Dealing with questions
Users often have questions on the use of information provisioning or how functions must be carried out. The business information administrator is the ideal person to answer these questions. For business information management, knowledge of the subject, and of the business process in relation to information provisioning is, therefore, essential. Based on questions, complaints, and the wishes of users, business information management also gets a specific insight into:
- How users deal with information provisioning and whether users can make proper use of information provisioning.
- The method by which information provisioning fits in with the business processes in practice.
- The extent to which information provisioning and information systems are used.
- Developments that occur in the business process.

The process of handling questions is important. Monitoring the procedure is important, but the key aspect is that answers are given to the questions. This requires knowledge of the subject, the business processes, and the supporting information provisioning.

The response to questions constantly leads to actions in other *management processes*. A question or a complaint can, for example, lead to the change of details or management data. A question can also lead to actions required from the IT providers, for example by submitting a change request. *End user support*, therefore, to a great extent shapes the face of the entire business information management.

Proactive communication
Through the use of proactive communication, business information management can also influence and optimize the use of information provisioning. By regular communications via newsletters, e-mail, Internet and other forms, business information management can inform users of changes in the IT services, developments that are underway, how information systems can be used more effectively, and ways in which information provisioning should not be used.

Pitfalls
End user support therefore creates the connection and the contact between business information management and the real business world. This is an important process for creating the right image. It is essential that the gap between users and business information management is small, or is perceived as being small.

Business information management was originally extremely close to the users and the function was in fact addressed directly by the users (which does not detract from the fact that there are also organizations where this arose from within IT). With reorganization, professionalization, or (re-) organization of business information management, there is a real risk of losing this close contact. This will mean losing the basis behind business information management. The effect of this will be that new business information managers and administrators will arise once again within the users.

From UPC practice
The first process adopted by the new business information management (BIM) group was that of *end user support*. Susan, interim head of the BIM group and Patrick's predecessor, was first to adopt this process based on past experiences. She was also involved with the organization of business information management in a previous role. On that occasion there was, following centralization of business information management at the company, poor communication between the new department and the end users, resulting in the latter carrying out their own business information management activities. Susan wanted to avoid that pitfall this time. Therefore she directly started setting up the *end user support* process. She began with the process of handling questions. She wanted to avoid users not getting any answers or receiving late responses to their questions.

By setting up agreements, she also wanted to guarantee that the business information managers and administrators gained and maintained knowledge of the business processes and any associated developments. Not every business information manager was convinced that this was necessary. They eventually went ahead on this basis but Susan knew from experience that it was difficult to keep knowledge updated when you are no longer working alongside the end users. In order to increase the responsiveness over the entire range of business processes, many questions with the associated answers were documented in the FAQ book (Frequently Asked Questions Book) which was published via the intranet. This meant that users could often find the answers to their questions themselves. In addition rigid management ensured that the gap between business information management and the users did not get too big, which was important. The result was that the business information managers and administrators became the ears and eyes in the area of information provisioning for the management.

The second action was organizing proactive communication. Susan prepared a newsletter that was distributed twice a week, via e-mail and the intranet. This outlined future developments, sometimes providing a forum for users, frequently asked questions and including tips and tricks.

Now that the BIM group is three years older, it is becoming more difficult to put together the newsletter on such a regular basis, though there are still several developments such as the on-going standardization of the business processes that can be included. Patrick took the decision a year ago to reduce the frequency of the newsletter to once a month.

A further initiative was the SAG web (Subscription and Advertisement users Group) and the user days. This was not initiated by Susan as she had left to start a new job two years ago, but by her successor Patrick who subsequently delegated it to Cathy as she had worked closely with Susan in this area.

Things still do not go entirely smoothly. Attendance at the first user's day was a little disappointing and also the SAG web only received a few visits. Perhaps the reorganization within the user organization has played a part in this.

However, the most important objectives have been achieved: the gap between users and business information management is still small, despite most users being at other locations. As a result, Susan has achieved her primary objective and has happily moved on to a new organization that is just a bike ride away from her house.

3.3   Business data management

Objective of business data management
In the process *business data management,* the data in information provisioning (or business information) is of central importance. Several demands are placed on this business information: it must be correct, support the business process, and also enable management of this business process.
The role of business information management is important in this:

- Some data is so crucial for the operational management that normal users may not alter it, for example, VAT percentages or step tariffs. The alteration of this data is a task often incumbent on business information management.
- The correctness and topicality of data in information provisioning must be guaranteed as far as possible. There is,

therefore, a supervisory responsibility that demands a deep knowledge of the data and the business information model.
- Management and users can request information that is not readily available from information provisioning. Answering these questions demands significant knowledge of the data, its precise meaning, and coherence. It also demands time to analyze and answer the questions.

These activities take place within business data management. There are, therefore, generally three types of activities:
- *Changing* (critical) data and not regularly correcting regular data.
- *Checking* data and data collection (including relations with the data model) and checking the results of data processing.
- *Reporting* and management reports including providing extra details such as ad hoc management information.

Information and data
Business data management deals with both automated and non-automated information provisioning. Automated often means an information system (application). Non-automated is similar to card-index boxes, spreadsheets (Excel), or paper lists, etc.

This information provisioning distinguishes between two sorts of data:
- Management data – this is the data in information provisioning with which the results and working of information provisioning for the business process are managed and updated. Intrinsic management data determines the outcome of the results of information provisioning for the business process (for example, VAT percentage, amounts whereby the first table (scale) of discount (pace list) applies).

Non-intrinsic management data determines the working of information provisioning or the way in which results are calculated (for example, whether or not they are delivered to the tax authorities, extra security necessary).

- Regular data – also contains information provisioning, as well as normal data such as orders, subscriptions, and name and address details. This data must be up-to-date, correct, consistent, and complete. Much of this is extracted from controls within automated information systems.

For both types of data, business information management has another role. Regular data is entered and amended by the (end-) users. Business information management has the role of monitoring the correctness (if possible) as well as the consistency.

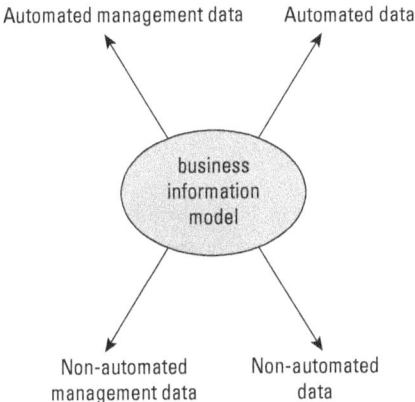

Figure 10 Data in information provisioning

Also the non-regular change of the data (it must be 'tinkered with' to improve it) comes under the activities. The latter is of course undesired but cannot always be avoided: users sometimes make mistakes and the information system seldom intercepts all possible mistakes. Also, there are often several information systems working alongside one another and the data used between these systems is not always consistent.

The coherence of all this is described in the (business) information model. This is the description with which the various types of information and data of the organization are displayed, including demands on this information and the mutual coherence. This is often not explicitly available and is in peoples' heads. For the preparation of management information, it is essential that this model is made more explicit.

From UPC practice
In contrast to *end user support*, which was previously grouped together with the intention of moving more 'towards the business side of things', *business data management* was grouped together at a later date. Until then, experienced users within the various publishers had carried out many of these activities.

Only last year did consideration for the correctness of data arise. Within UPC there was an enormous need for management information, together with a structured approach for providing this. An incident the previous summer speeded up this requirement for a more structured process enormously. A new user who was replacing a colleague during the holidays had adapted the subscription rates for an edition. However, he mistakenly entered the rates too high with the result that, as it was not noticed, invoices were sent that were much too high. The Board of Directors demanded clarification and the introduction of measures to prevent this happening again, mainly due to the fact that competitor newspapers had been running reports of the incident on their front pages for two days.

A second reason was that in handling the incident, great difficulty was experienced due to the contamination of the details in the subscriptions- and distribution data. Also, it was not discovered until then how many difficulties were experienced by both users and suppliers as a result of working with this incorrect data. Edgar Morrison was tasked by Patrick to deal with this.

After thorough analysis, Edgar arrived at a plan involving a number of action points and phases.

- The first was the close-down of hazardous functions and the securing of sensitive data.
- The second was developing agreements for changing this data.
- The third was rectifying the incorrect data. Edgar knew that correcting this would be a long-term project as it was not known which data was incorrect. Dealing with this would take a lot of time and capacity and must take place in a project-based manner.
- Edgar also recognized there were many demands for management information but there was not much sense in doing much without knowing which data was correct. Correcting the management information was therefore the fourth point.

The first action was quite easy. With the help of the authorization modules from PARIS (see Annex 1 for explanation), it was simple for Edgar to complete data for users and only provide the alteration procedures to a limited group (business information administrators). This meant he had brought the extremely critical data into a managed situation. Edgar then set up procedures for changing this data. This also took care of point two.

The third stage focused upon improving the quality of information. The first part of this was dealt with in business information management, the second has become a separate project.

The first part has led to the introduction of measures for detecting as far as possible any incorrect data in the system by means of set problems in the system and the use of check counts.

The actual correcting of the data by contacting subscribers has become another project, separate from business information management. Based on checklists (containing questionable cases), the subscriber will receive a telephone call to see if the data is still correct. Edgar has had two temporary staff hired for this.

Edgar already saw that something had to be done with the management information but on the management level, this has only been up-to-date for sixth months. Edgar has started the MI project by listing the questions asked earlier. He separated the seldom-asked questions (including queries), and has documented and grouped the more frequently asked questions in the so-called MI kit. In order to provide appropriate answers to the questions, he has set up a process in which a structured search is carried out as to whether this question has been asked already so that the reuse of previous responses is possible. Structural consideration is also paid to the intake of these information questions.

As well as this phase, the MI project was started. In this project, a data warehouse was developed so the questions can be answered much easier and faster. In the past, many MI questions were answered by VGK (see Annex 1 for explanation) by way of queries. This was an expensive and time-consuming solution. Edgar is still looking for an environment for this project.

3.4 Operational supplier management

An important part of the activities of *use management* within business information management consists of the *operational supplier management* process. The objective of the *operational supplier management* process is giving operational orders to the IT providers and monitoring the working of automated information provisioning and the IT providers.

Operational management of suppliers deals with three subjects (see also Chapter 6, *management processes* cluster):
- Services – the IT provider provides (agreed) services in the area of information provisioning, for example, keeping work places operational and running the order system.
- Products – these services (or those from assignments given) lead to outputs. Examples are a series of printed invoices, electronic transfers, product overviews, or debtor lists.
- Assignments – not all products and services are identified or contractually agreed in advance. Business information management often gives additional assignments, for example, deviations from the agreed services (such as extended opening for online processing), additional services (such as extra support in the case of an extended migration), or other products (such as starting incidental processing).

Business information management provides support in these areas with three activities:

- Planning – this mainly states when and how the services must be carried out and stipulates which requirements the existing, incidental or new services must satisfy. The IT supplier is, therefore, given information so that they can also keep the operational services up to standard in the future. An example of this is stating the estimated needs for changes in the business process, thereby indicating the desired performance of the information system for the future.
- Providing – issuing of service requests, for example, for incidental processing or for changes in the services.
- Monitoring – checking that the services and products delivered conform to the agreement (such as a service level agreement) and whether the orders have been, or are being, carried out.

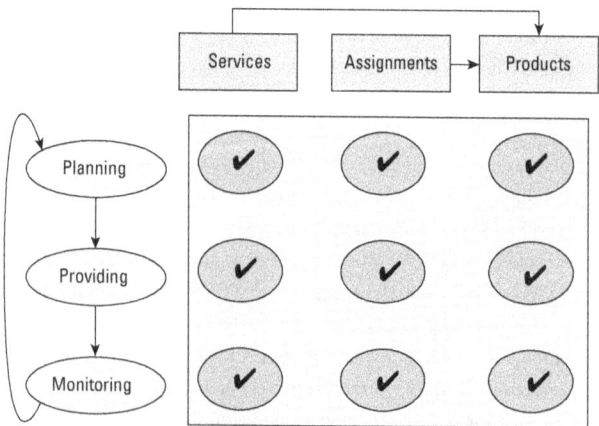

Figure 11 Activities within the operational supplier management process

Business information management therefore also has a strong controlling and monitoring task regarding the IT providers and the IT services. There are often agreements with IT providers in which it is established that they will periodically report on the realization of the operational services, possibly relating to the agreed service levels. Business information management will look at these service level reports. All this leads to the *operational supplier management* process being closely related to and realizing what is laid down in the *contract management* process.

From UPC practice
Operational supplier management was the second process within *use management* that UPC dealt with. Because VGK formalized the processing, they also needed a central contact point within UPC. VGK had previously complained about the situation in UPC whereby different departments often issued different orders, which resulted in problems as VGK did not know which orders had priority and those that could wait. This led to the establishment of a contact point within UPC.

Bert, and later Maria were given this task by Susan. The fact that the *end user support* process started working was an enormous help. More and more people within UPC found their way to business information management.

Susan was in a rush to organize this process, as there were quite a few mistakes in the processing that had annoying consequences as UPC had set up the wrong processing parameters. All publishers set up the parameters themselves and it turned out that the knowledge was not up-to-date in all locations. It was initially thought that the mistake was in the computer program and arrangements were made for VGK to check this out. Unfortunately, the VGK administrators were able to show that the mistake was caused by an incorrect parameter and this resulted in an extra invoice being sent out. It was therefore definitely necessary to start managing and controlling this activity centrally.

As a continuation of what VGK was doing, Bert began streamlining the control of the processing. The first thing he did was to map out the current processing activities for UPC, when they had to be undertaken, and what the purpose of each was. He also documented the parameters used for this. It was amusing to see that in some cases completely different processing activities were used for almost the same result.

Bert also realized that various processing activities could be carried out by VGK just as well without written permission from UPC and that UPC just hampered the process. These were processing activities of a purely technical nature. He has subsequently put this to *contract management*.

The next step was to monitor and control the results of this for which he created an MS Access application so that he could view the processing activities that had to be run on a daily basis.

Bert then set about establishing the processes for the non-regular processing activities. This failed the first time as Bert himself made a mistake in his application. When these problems were resolved, he extended the processes to cover all (operational) questions to and orders for VGK.

He then concentrated on the disturbances. VGK had acquired a bad reputation in parts of the organization due to the regular disturbances that had occurred in the past and which were also occurring now. Bert therefore began to create a summary of all the disturbances partly with the help of information provided by VGK.

It turned out that the number of disturbances was not as high as expected. Furthermore, some were caused by UPC itself due to the entry of the wrong parameters, though this had already been discovered.

He now deals with the service level reports. VGK reports monthly on the development, management and maintenance activities they undertake and these are lengthy reports incorporating all kinds of service levels. It takes Bert a considerable amount of time to read these and he is unsure of the added value that these reports provide.

Slowly, the discovery has been made within UPC that some things may take place less formally and intensively. The annoying thing is that it was, of all people, a consultant tasked by the Board of Directors of UPC who demanded these reports on the service levels. Bert made a suggestion to *contract management* that he should speak with VGK about this. To his surprise, this went down extremely well, since it transpired that VGK also had concerns with the level of these reports.

4 Functionality management cluster

4.1 Introduction

The second group of processes within BiSL is the *functionality management* cluster. The objective of *functionality management* is initiating changes and ensuring that these changes are worked out in a functional information process. Within *functionality management*, the completion of information provisioning is determined both for the automated and the non-automated.

We recognize four processes within the *functionality management* cluster. Two of these are aimed at the design (desired change) of information provisioning and two are aimed at the preparation/realization of the change.

The four processes are:
- *Specify information requirements*– the design of automated information provisioning or the changes in this information provisioning.
- *Design non-automated information systems*– the design of the non-automated information provisioning and the means for this.
- *Review and testing*– validating the solution and realized (changed) information provisioning.
- *Prepare transition* – preparing for the implementation of information provisioning and the desired changes in the user organization.

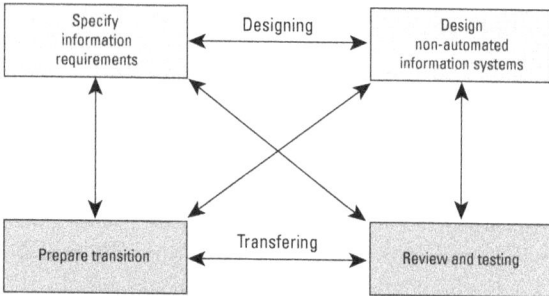

Figure 12 The processes within the functionality management cluster

4.2   Specify information requirements

The several objectives of specify information requirements
'Think before you do' is the credo forming the basis of *specify information requirements*. 'A good beginning is half the work' also fits in well here. The objective of this process is translating and laying down (by *change management*, part of the *connecting processes) of* the desired functionality changes into a solution so that IT providers can realize these requirements. In other words, formulating the requirement put to the IT provider. Its clarity and correctness must also be such that clear acceptance of the solution delivered by the IT provider is possible.

The *specify information* requirements process therefore has several objectives:
- Clarifying the requirement: is the requirement correct, does it make sense and what are the frameworks surrounding the requirement.
- Considering solution directions, choosing a solution and giving feedback on this to the initiating *change management* and if necessary to the decision-making processes.

- Detailing and laying down this solution in specifications.
- Validating the correctness of the selected solution and the specifications.

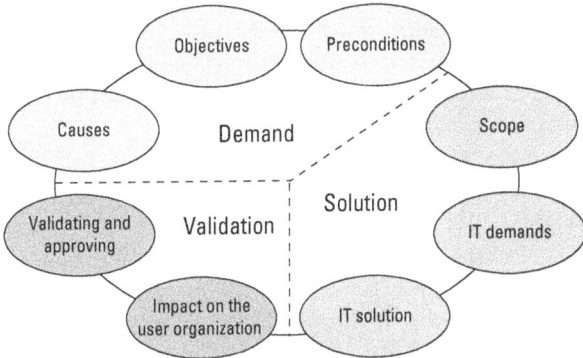

Figure 13 Subjects in the specify information requirements process

A desired change goes through a number of stages within *specify information requirements:* from the needs via the solution to the validation.

The demand
The first step in the process is clarifying the need for information provisioning or changes to it. A good knowledge of the problem is half the solution. Therefore, the *specify information requirements* process starts with recognizing and mapping out the environment of the change request. For this, we shall go into more details regarding:

- Causes – why is there the need for change and what are the reasons behind this.

- Objectives – what exactly does one envisage achieving with the change, what must be achieved with the change, what are the objectives and do these solve the requirement.
- Frameworks and preconditions – which frameworks and preconditions are there that the solution direction must satisfy such as financial frameworks, frameworks regarding solutions (information policy), personnel frameworks. See also the *demand management* process.

The solution

All roads lead to Rome. The second step in the process is determining the solution space, the various solution directions and the choice of the solution:

- Scope of the solution– the area in information provisioning in which the solution must be sought and the solution directions that are possible.
- IT demands or specifications – the demands placed on the automated part of the information provisioning, or the desired changes to the existing IT.
- IT solution – the description based on the specifications of the solution by the IT provider. Often also called the design.

Validation and approval

The considered and selected solution direction must of course also be validated as far as the organization and environment are concerned. The selected solution must fit within the organization and its methods. Validation must also be carried out into feasibility, impact, possibility of success, completeness and costs of the solution, thus creating support for it. The validation of the specification (or more often of the design to be approved) is very important: finally, this is the official document that forms the basis upon which the acceptance of the solution takes place.

Impact
During the *specify information requirements* process, the effectiveness of the solution will be determined, as well as the ambition level and the completion of the solution. The quality of the specification therefore has great influence on the costs and the benefits of information provisioning.

Carrying out this process, therefore, differs from situation to situation. Sometimes it is necessary to develop several solution directions in order to clarify the final needs, or to discover that something else is desired. Sometimes, a solution direction must be clear to a reasonable level of detail in order to discover whether this covers a need or not. The supplier also often has knowledge of the business process and can, therefore, give recommendations on how the requirement can be best met or provide further suggestions on possible solutions.

Solution directions influence the needs and the associated frameworks and expectations (such as available budget, envisaged delivery date). The needs influence the offer, which in turn influences the needs. It therefore often happens that during the *specify information requirements* process, one must return to the person who originally formulated the requirement, be the management or the supplier.

From UPC practice
In the past UPC used to rely heavily on VGK with regard to the *specify information requirements* process. Also, the entire process of specifying information requirements must have

been extremely confusing for VGK as they received
various changes and requests for change from different
UPC locations. Even if this involved essentially the same
functionality, there were minor differences. It also turned
out that certain changes had unintentional effects on the
processes within other parts of PARIS, which in turn caused
more problems within UPC.

As VGK is going to operate more and more as a package
owner, UPC's influence on specifying the functionality
of PARIS will be smaller and they will have less control.
Nevertheless, two-and-a half years ago, a place was
designated within UPC where the specifications for changes
in PARIS would be made. This was not without a struggle,
as some publishers of departments were afraid that their
requirements would no longer be specified accurately.
However, after it was agreed that specifications would always
be approved by the publisher or department that submitted
the requirement, everyone seemed reasonably happy in the
organization.

Brian Woodman was tasked by Susan to act as the contact
point for VGK. He is well known at VGK as, in the past, he
was intensively involved from a UPC perspective in a number
of large releases. The first project he was involved with was
intended to clarify the objectives behind the decision to
develop the specifications for changes in PARIS in-house.
The situation is that the role of UPC and their influence
on the functionality on PARIS is less and less, especially
now that VGK is going to operate increasingly as a package
supplier and has also set up its own product management
department

There are however still enough reasons for making clear specifications. It seemed easy on one or two occasions for Brian to create plain and clear specifications so that agreement could be achieved internally within UPC as to the desired changes. Another important objective is clarifying, why changes are desired and whether there are no other possible solutions apart from adjustments to PARIS. By looking at the requirement in a more structured manner and paying more attention to the causes, objectives, and preconditions, Brian has gained a better insight into the various solution directions, and the costs and benefits of these.

Brian has created a step-by-step plan in order to complete the process. He has also developed a standard template for specifications. The administrative procedures used in the organization are receiving more attention from Brian as part of the *specify information requirements* process. The ways in which PARIS is used differs a fair bit between different users and departments. Many users and some administrators are not sufficiently up-to-date on all possibilities that the package offers.

As part of the template he has, therefore, explicitly reserved room in which the main points of the change are included for the administrative process.

Setting up the specifications was quite difficult in the first year: there were many local methods and this often led to difficult discussions. However, with the combination of business information management and the business departments there is more standardization in the business process. Brian believes that the organization of the specification process has played a big part in this.

The conclusion was also frequently reached that some changes could be implemented normally into the administrative process or, better, into other parts of the information provisioning. The process slowly gained stability. Brian has also already transferred the templates to the business information management clubs for the other parts of the information provisioning.

4.3   Design non-automated information systems

With information provisioning, we quickly think of the information systems themselves and the underlying technical infrastructure. For many managers and users, the term 'information provisioning' is itself synonymous with the information systems used and often even with underlying technology such as Oracle, SAP or .NET. Less noticeable, but actually important is the non-automated part of information provisioning.

Designing non-automated information provisioning
Non-automated information provisioning is the implementation of processes of information provisioning that are not automated. This non-automated information provisioning includes elements such as:
• User guides – descriptions, stating how the (automated) information system must be used in information process.

- Procedure descriptions and work instructions – descriptions as to what form information provisioning or information processing procedures should take.
- Non-automated or semi-automated administration – paper lists, spreadsheets, electronic card-index box, and supporting aids such as forms, etc.
- Methods and agreements – how to deal with information and information systems, whether or not they are documented.

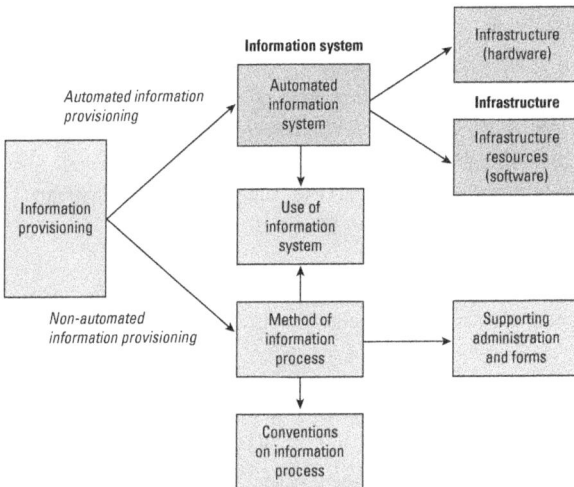

Figure 14 The connection between automated and non-automated information provisioning

This information provisioning should, just like the automated version, be designed, described, realized, tested, and transferred to management. This takes place in the *design non-automated information systems* process with the main aspects of this being determined within the *specify information requirements* process.

It is clear that there must be relations and coherence between the automated and non-automated parts of the information provisioning. Non-automated information provisioning is often also a buffer and overspill for automated information provisioning, due to the fact that, for example:

- Functionality that is too expensive or too uncommon is not built into the (automated) information system. Users must be aware of this and carry out this functionality.
- Functionality that is too complex (for a computer), or for which additional (not established or structured) information is necessary must be carried out by users.
- Automated information systems are rarely capable of enforcing all limitations, norms and other things. Users therefore often also carry out other controls (such as for example, within social services, where a lot of time is spent checking on the legality of benefits).

In close coordination with the *specify information requirements* process, the non-automated information provisioning is designed and established in the following steps:

- Determining the objectives, preconditions, basic points of the (not-automated) information provisioning and determining the global solution.
- Determining relations and connections with the automated information provisioning and establishing where the non-automated information provisioning must offer completion and additional features such as extra coding systems, extra process- or control steps, and additional non-automated administration.
- Working out the non-automated information processes and associated forms, etc.

- Laying down this process, so that users know of and are able to work with the new or changed method.

From UPC practice

Research carried out by Bert and Andrew Jones into improvement of the management of the business information, and tests on the user manual within the review and test procedure showed that the user manuals were very poor.

When Patrick gave Andrew the order to bring some clarity into the situation, it turned out things were actually worse. The view of the business processes was very limited: users were able to work very efficiently with PARIS but nobody knew why they did certain things.

When Andrew asked how a certain subscription was to be entered, it was possible to provide an answer stating how it was done (first function fast code A22, then enter the data with subscription code B110, etc.) but nobody knew why it was done in this way. Checks were also carried out without knowing what was actually being checked.

Furthermore, some people appeared to be unfamiliar with new features and functionality. Indeed, with every new release, there was a statement saying what new features PARIS offered but nobody could find these as the user manuals had not been updated for some time.

The rationale behind certain actions, checks or agreements was therefore slightly lost. More annoying still was that the actions were still to a large extent determined by the past. For example in one part of UPC, there were different system uses and agreements than with the other parts.

Andrew was also shocked at the inconsistencies between the system and the administrative organization. The form used for 'change of address' turned out to be completely the other way round from the on-screen form. The screen on the website appeared to somewhere in between these two. Not too far-reaching research into the user manuals and procedure descriptions quickly resulted in a list of no fewer than 248 inconsistencies or mistakes.

It is clear that this will mean a lot of work but it is important that the mistakes are rectified. It is a challenge for Andrew as it the work is in addition to his regular activities of reviewing and testing of releases.

Andrew's intentions are to establish and optimize the various administrative processes. He cannot manage this alone but will have to enter into close negotiations with the various users and user groups. An extra complication is that the necessary differences have occurred as a result of how the various groups of users work.

This means that standardization will take some time, and as the reorganization is still underway, it will not proceed quickly. Andrew therefore has started some preliminary work with a colleague. They have developed a template for process descriptions (containing an explicit consideration for the 'why') and they have started work on a process for changes in the non-automated information provisioning. Following on from that process, Andrew and his colleague started on some manual administrations, changing forms and screens with a view to solving the most annoying mistakes. In order to maintain control of the entire process, this takes place via *change management*. He has still not included the 248 changes in the change requests: this makes the whole process a little complex. Furthermore, the list is still not exhaustive as there are various other mistakes and inconsistencies that have still not been described.

Andrew still does not know how all of this is to be put straight. Time will tell, he hopes.

4.4   Review and testing

Objective
The *review and testing* process ensures that desired changes to information provisioning are carried out in an approved manner within the organization and that the instruments used, as well as the aids and support, function correctly. This is why the various products in the area of information provisioning are reviewed and tested for correctness and coherence, with the objective of achieving correct functional information provisioning. It is also important to be able to detect and rectify any mistakes and shortcomings on time.

Subjects
Here, we look at the correctness and coherence of various subjects such as:

- Automated information provisioning – an important part here is the (user-) acceptance test, the test whereby business information management checks to see if the IT provider has delivered everything that has been agreed and whether this works correctly.
- Non-automated information provisioning – a check is carried out to see if the non-automated part fits in with the automated part, if the use of the entire information system fits in with the business process, the need for change, and whether everything fulfils the changes stated.
- User organization – the selected solution and change must fit in with the user organization.
- Transition plan – the new information provisioning or the changed version of the information provisioning leads to changes. The transition plan describes the steps of the change. These steps must be consistent with the changes and the chosen solutions.

The acceptance test

The most visible product of *review and testing* is the acceptance test; this is the means by which a user organization grants sign-off to an IT organization. The starting point for the acceptance test are the specifications or the designs based on this (and approved by business information management). The acceptance test is used to check whether the changed or the delivered information system and/or underlying technical infrastructure perform as agreed in these documents. A good specification or design is therefore important. A good acceptance test is very important: this is often the basis of sign-off being granted to the contractor and responsibility for the working of the new version or the new system being accepted by the user organization.

Information system and structure

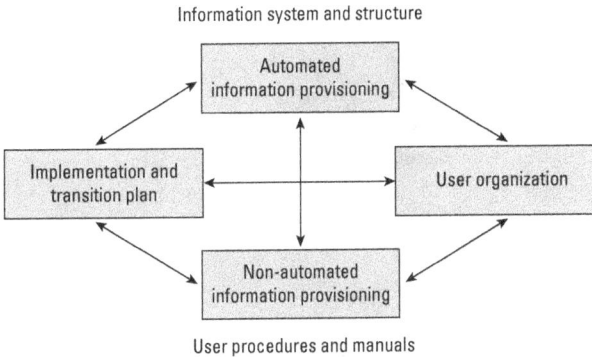

User procedures and manuals

Figure 15 The subjects within review and testing

In practice, often less consideration is given to subjects other than testing the new version of the application. That's why the connection between working methods in the business process and in the IT is sometimes poor and one sometimes uses information provisioning in a non-uniform manner. In the case of centralizations, fusions, and consolidations, these differences then come to light and become a hindrance. Also in the case of other developments such as for example, when new systematic way of working is introduced or when selecting a new information system, bad connection is a hindrance.

From UPC practice
Acceptance tests were one of the things that UPC had sorted out at an early stage. Once or twice in the distant past, untested releases were taken into production with drastic consequences. This resulted in no more untested releases being taken into production. The acceptance test procedure was the first procedure that UPC introduced in the area of business information management.

It only became clear a year ago that the process of acceptance tests was however still not complete when a new overview was delivered by the advertising department. VGK delivered and tested the subsequent release in perfect condition. No mistakes were discovered in the acceptance test by UPC. However, when the new release was introduced into the production departments, it was noticed that it took a very long time to create a list, which jeopardized the production and delivery of the newspaper.

It was clear that the test criteria were not complete and neither were the acceptance criteria or the specifications, so work was started on this.

The subject was then left as there were other priorities. However, it again caught Andrew's attention, as the manager of the review and test process, following developments in the improvement of business information management.

Andrew noted that the user manuals were far from good and discovered that this was partly caused by the fact that they were not being updated. He came across this by chance, as the users had made mistakes when entering data resulting in complaints from subscribers and consequently an update of the database by VGK. In the case of another business information management group, for the financial system, the user manual was updated following a release. It included a step-by-step description of how to enter an invoice. However, as the writer had forgotten to carry out one of the steps, probably due to fatigue bearing in mind it was just before he went on holiday, nobody was able to work with it. This led to he went on holiday, nobody was able to work with it. This led to a change in the test procedure at UPC; internal user manuals and work instructions were to be included in the test from now on.

Research has, however, shown that the user manuals contain many inconsistencies and mistakes. The last delivered release is currently being tested by UPC and Andrew is well aware that he will never make the delivery date if he has to resolve all mistakes known to date, or rather has them solved in the *design non-automated information systems* process.

Andrew has therefore agreed with Patrick to concentrate for now on those parts of the user manual that have been updated for this release. Fortunately, this is more achievable.

In addition, after consultation with Patrick, Andrew has agreed to also include the implementation plan and the transition plans in the acceptance test procedure but it will still take some time before this step is taken. The process is now working reasonably well and it may be that it takes some unexpected mishap in order to move on to the next step. Not that Andrew has a problem with this: priorities have to be set and sometimes change must come about as the result of unexpected events.

4.5   Prepare transition

The fourth process within the *functionality management* cluster is *prepare transition*. Transition is in practice often also called implementation but this word has several meanings, including programming and installing. The objective of the *prepare*

Organization		Information provision
IT services	IT	Automated IT
Business info. mgt org.	Business info. mgt.	Data
User organization	Business/ organization	Users

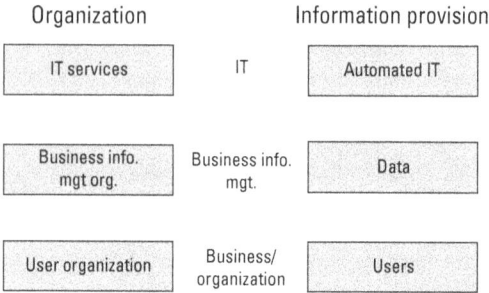

Figure 16 Relevant subjects within a transition

transition process is to enable a problem-free adoption of the new or changed information provisioning by completing all necessary (operational) preconditions in advance of their recognition.

These preconditions and changes refer both to information provisioning and its organization. Examples of possible changes to be carried out before or during a transition are:

- Agreements must be made or amended regarding availability, performance of the new release and/or the activities that the IT organization must carry out.
- The business information management organization can also undergo changes in work. So, for example, for each new release, the financial summary must be viewed and controlled before it is sent to the managers involved.
- Changes can also take place in the user organization. For example, through the link with the marketing data, there are new agreements as to who is responsible for what data.

- Due to the change, conversions may be necessary and a lot of these are carried out automatically. The IT organization undertakes this but the old version must also preserved, etc.
- The business information management organization will have to check these conversions and must also carry out various changes manually such as, for example, the functional system parameters.
- The new or changed information provisioning can involve changes for the users' methods. In the new situation users, for example, no longer need to use the tracking forms for checking outgoing invoices, but one must explicitly check the declared details with the use of the computer.

Diversity
There are very many subjects to consider during the transition and the *prepare transition* process is large and can differ on each occasion. This is to do with impact, time of carrying out, and location.

First of all, the impact or the nature of the change differs significantly for each occasion. Changes sometimes have hardly any impact on the user organization, since the only activities undertaken relate to IT work. Other changes are fundamental, users will start working completely differently and there are associated education and training requirements. A new information system or a new method can be introduced, resulting in widespread changes.

The complexity is increased further as the timing of the transition depends on the set-up of information provisioning (such as for example, during the *prepare transition* process or during the transition). Certain activities (such as data conversion) can sometimes take place initially prematurely but are not included in a following release. There is therefore no standard means of determining what must take place and when. Therefore, one of the products must also be the transition plan: a plan describing what must take place during transition.

It is also possible that a change is not carried out in one place but at various times, at several locations, in a single organization, or in various organizations. It is however desirable to do so as far in advance as possible so that the transition itself is as small as possible.

From UPC practice

In the past, a lot of mistakes were made when transferring new releases and entering new systems. We got to know about this and as a result a 'Don't forget' list was set up. This list hung on the notice board in the business information management room and was used as a reminder. The list was very extensive, not everything applied all the time but points of interest were put down on paper. This indeed meant nobody forgot anything but it was occasionally discovered at the last minute that something else had to be done. For example, it was realized at the last minute that a conversion had to be carried out which the users did not know anything about. This resulted in the helpdesk being inundated with all sorts of unnecessary questions and reports; it also meant that preparing the transition was undertaken poorly.

VGK took over the production of the conversion software itself due to problems with conversions. Much to the delight of UPC: something less to worry about! Due to problems with the e-release, Patrick decided to improve the *transition management* and *prepare transition* processes jointly and in accelerated mode. Because Brian had successfully adopted the specification process, Patrick decided to give him this assignment.

Brian has started work on the Don't forget list and is looking to see which activities could be carried out early. He has a standard plan for the *prepare transition* process, with additional procedures for coordination with user departments and the IT functions.
He has also split up the Don't forget list according to activities and subjects that play a role within the *prepare transition* process, within the *transition management* process, or are dependent upon the situation within both of these.

All of this has resulted in better planning. Brian does, however, note that the wheel is still being re-invented as far as various entries to the Don't forget list are concerned. Also, the way in which people do things is often different.

For the forthcoming year, he intends to investigate this further, with the intention of ensuring that the process can proceed more efficiently.

He has, for example, the idea that communicating to the users, such as having the training and the information take place more along the same lines, so that the users can find the relevant information faster. For the information, he currently uses the Users' Change Newsletter issued by the VGK in HTML format so that it can be published on the Intranet.

5 Connecting processes cluster

5.1 Introduction

Between the clusters *use management* and *functionality management,* we have the *connecting processes.* The processes in this cluster ensure the synchronization between *functionality management* and *use management.* They ensure that from the organization of the business process, desired changes are listed, initiated if necessary, and implemented in the user organization(s) after the changes have been completed.

There are two processes in this cluster (see also Annex 5):
* *Change management* – recognizing and deciding which changes are to be carried out and initiating the change.
* *Transition management* – carrying out (implementing) the change in the user organization.

We can therefore summarize the objective behind the *connecting processes* as initiating and ending (carrying out/realization) of the change.

5.2 Change management

Objective
The main objective of *change management* is arriving at the correct decision regarding the implementation of changes or renewals in information provisioning. A second objective, in addition to carrying out this decision-making, is to provide an assembly point for change requests. In *change management,*

needs and requests for changes are administered, analyzed, prioritized, and initiated depending on the decision-making. Issuing the order and realizing a change proceeds via *contract management*. *Contract management* issues orders to IT.

There are, therefore, two activities within *change management*:
- Receiving and administering the changes and providing feedback.
- Organizing and carrying out the decision-making.

Change management together with *specify information requirements* defines to a great extent the costs and effectiveness of information provisioning. Correct decision-making in relation to changes has a significant effect on the costs, quality, effectiveness, and future-proofing of information provisioning:
- By carrying out *change management* effectively, it is possible to identify and therefore proceed with unnecessary, superfluous, or unimportant change requests, so that these types of change are not implemented and therefore need not be paid for.
- Efficient prioritizing makes it possible to carry out the important changes in good time and the less important ones later. This also makes it possible to manage the benefits of information provisioning and their effectiveness in the business process.
- Effective planning in releases also enables changes to be carried out more efficiently, for example, by combining issues. This also reduces the costs of changes.

It is, therefore, important to have an insight into why the change is desirable or necessary, and what the requirement is. In administering a change, one must therefore keep updated the

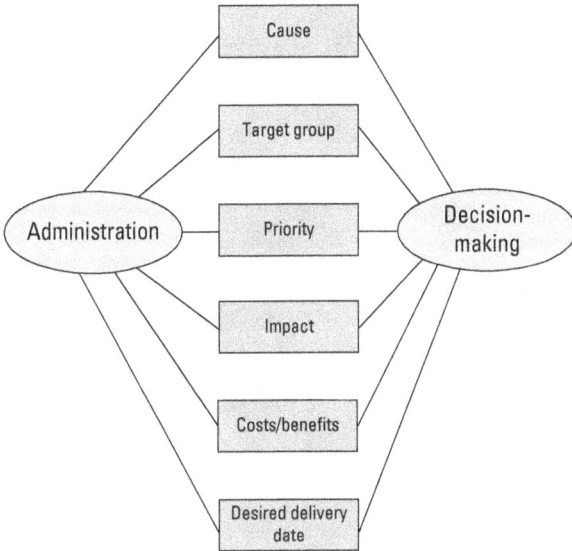

Figure 17 Aspects of change management

various characteristics of the change request such as why the request was initiated, the person making the request, the target group, necessity/priority, and desired delivery date.

Change management is closely connected with *specify information requirements*. *Change management* deals with the question of whether anything has to change regarding information provisioning. When specifying information requirements, the solution is designed and coordinated to the needs and the frameworks. Whether a change is desired also depends on the shape this will take. This is why feedback is given continually between *change management* and *specify information requirements*. For example, as part of the first step within *specify*

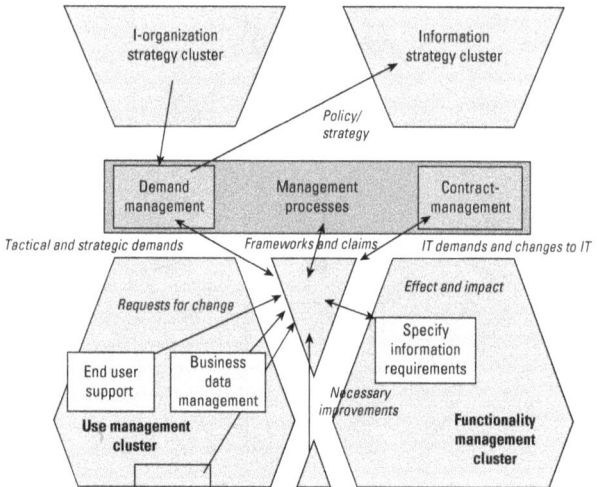

Figure 18 The central position of change management

information requirements, causes, problems and objectives
are determined and worked out further. The solution and the
associated cost estimates are also outlined. The characteristics
identified by this step are not always the same as those with which
one started. Feedback is then of course provided.

Change requests come from several quarters. As well as
requests from users and business information managers and
administrators (via the *use management* processes), it is possible,
for example, that requests will also be placed on the agenda
from developments and policy (*demand management*), as a
result of changes in the law, from the IT department, and even
from *functionality management* (for example, if specifications
and therefore solutions have not entirely delivered what was

required). Figure 18 illustrates this practice, which can often appear chaotic.

Where it is decided that changes have to be carried out, they are conveyed via *contract management* to the IT function. Here, processes such as *change management* have often been implemented in order to plan and carry out the change in the plans. One should not confuse this change management process with the BiSL *change management* process.

> **From UPC practice**
> When Patrick Everts was appointed as Susan's successor two years ago and placed in charge of the BIM group for the subscriptions and the advertising administration, he first started working on *change management*. He immediately recognized the central role of *change management* within business information management and also its importance for information provisioning.
>
> He believed that if you wish to know what is happening, you must know what has to be changed. He was motivated here by Mohammed Saleh from VGK who was also involved in bringing this process up to standard within VGK. Patrick quickly realized that much was at stake at UPC and that it was a mess. All UPC departments sent their changes directly to VGK, there was no prioritizing, some changes appeared completely superfluous or conflicting, and there were sometimes conflicting objectives.

It took Patrick a great deal of time and effort to streamline this and to have all change requests processed via one central point. Fortunately, VGK assisted in this, for example, by sending all change requests from UPC on to Patrick and waiting for his response before undertaking any work at VGK.

This helped Patrick to achieve his first objective, i.e., centralizing all change requests, gaining an insight into these and being able to manage the process. He also quickly achieved his second objective, i.e., setting up a procedure for submitting change requests. The latter still appeared to be quite a problem mainly because management initially seemed completely uninterested in sticking to new agreements. With the support of the Board of Directors, however, he managed to gain control of this.

Part of this procedure also involved introducing a template for change requests in which consideration had to be given to causes, problems, priorities, desired delivery dates, estimated costs, and benefits. Patrick created the shortened intake procedure in order to be able to process and carry out a first validation on this. Business information administrators take a look at the request, possibly supported by VGK, and causes and costs are refined and often also changed.

A pleasing effect of this procedure was a rather steep decline in the number of change requests. This caused some grumbling in the organization but the Board of Directors was quite satisfied. It was gradually understood that that a lot of strange and unimportant things had been requested in the past.

A third step that Patrick was also able to take quickly was the agreement to streamline and formalize the decision-making process within the organization. He introduced the change calendar, which he had placed on the agenda in periodical consultation with Board of Directors and the management. Efficient planning of releases was also considered in conjunction with VGK.

The re-structuring of UPC has been undertaken whereby the number of locations from where requests are made has been significantly reduced. The situation within the business has thus become more transparent.

VGK has also assumed a more rigid role as package owner and introduces more and more priorities itself. This is logical as VGK has more clients.

On the other hand, UPC still has significant influence. This is partly because it is by far the biggest client of VGC, but also because the relations are very good between Patrick and Pilar Rodriguez, Mohammed Saleh's successor at VGC.

All of this led Patrick to consider transferring the *change management* process to Edgar so that he now had time left over for the more strategic processes and the more far-reaching standardization of business information management within UPC. All this effort regarding *change management* now seems less logical and relevant. Patrick knows this is not true. *Change management* is a central process and the many discussions and arguments were necessary in getting the commercialization and professionalization underway. The fact that things are now considerably quieter is also due to the fact that everyone realizes that information provisioning must be approached in a businesslike manner and that costs and benefits also play a role in information provisioning. Looking back on things, Patrick is happy that he started this. It was the key to getting the situation under control.

5.3   Transition management

Transition management is the second connecting process, which ensures that the (realized) changes in the information provisioning are carried out and implemented within the user organization and the business process. The result is operational information provisioning. Designed and prepared within *functionality management*, the changes are carried out (implemented) within *transition management*. The start of *transition management* lies therefore within *change management* and within *functionality management*. The last cluster contains the transition plan in which the activities to be carried out under *transition management* are stated.

Despite the changing character of *transition management* (every situation is new, see paragraph 4.5), some of the transition activities and steps certainly in a maintenance situation can easily be standardized in broad terms or in detail. It is possible and also desirable to have a set method, which is operated (for example, granting sign-off for the change). Having good checklists that specify further actions means that this process can be carried out in a considerably more structured manner.

Within *transition management*, there are three types of activities:

- Carrying out and continuing the changes such as, for example, implementing data conversions, having parameters entered, distributing information, or informing the users of the changes.
- Monitoring whether everything has been carried out, all measures have been taken, or all functions are ready (see Figure 19).
- Adjusting measures or taking additional measures if bottlenecks exist or occur.

	Organization	Contents	Transition
Business information management	• Organizing necessary business information management • Staffing business information management • Agreements	• Staffing user organization • System satisfies • Changes known • Documentation • Data collection	• Implementation plan • Users informed • Necessary agreements • Documentation distributed
Application management	• Organizing necessary application management processes • Staffing roles • Agreements	• Maintainable system • System test • Documentation	• Implementation plan • Data, duration • Capacity • Documentation distributed
IT infrastructure management	• Organizing necessary IT infrastructure management processes • Staffing roles • Agreements	• Performance test • Exploitation test • Documentation	• Implementation plan • Data, duration • Capacity • Documentation sent distributed

Figure 19 The nine areas of transition management

Within *transition management*, one must therefore verify whether changes and preconditions in the areas of organization, information provisioning (content), and the change phase (transition) have been carried out or fulfilled. This applies not only to the user organization (including business information management) but also whether the IT providers (application management and IT infrastructure management) have done so. See also Figure 19.

From UPC practice

The Don't forget list was the most important aid in *transition management*. In the past, after experience had been gained, the list was made up to prevent people forgetting things.

Brian had heard of a situation, though he was not sure if it was true, where for two months a new release had been installed but because UPC had not put the signature on the transfer form and returned it, VGK had not handed over the release for production.

In any case, because the list worked quite well, few other things were forgotten. Not many more things went wrong in carrying out the (real) activities of the *transition management* process, but there were still regular cases of people realizing at the last moment that things were not carried out meaning that plans were regularly not achieved. Following the cause of the problems with the e-release, Brian has adopted the processes *prepare transition* and *transition management*, and has decided to improve the necessary items. The transitions generally proceed well but this is mainly due to people's experience. The unexpected departure of Julie who after ten years of business information management moved to an IT business again made it painfully clear how dependent we were on human knowledge.

Maria, a highly experienced user took over Julie's work but in the area of *transition management*, she could not actually do anything. The Don't forget list stated what was to be done but often not how this was to be done and who should be involved. Brian ensured that in the new method a transition plan is included in the preparing of the transition, which outlines the steps to be taken during the transition. Many of these steps have been standardized. He therefore drew up the transition book. This is a handbook describing how things are to be done with respect to standard activities, what to pay attention to, and any forms that are to be used.

The transition plan refers to many of these activities. This means *transition management* is still not completely independent of personal input but the situation has been enormously improved. Brian actually believes that for all processes of business information management, the level of the *transition management* process should be achieved. This will probably not happen.

6 Management processes cluster

6.1 Introduction

The *management processes* cluster within BiSL includes the processes that deal with management on four subjects, i.e., the content and functionality (what), the costs and benefits (how much), the time and capacity (who and when) and the supply and automated IT (how and with what).

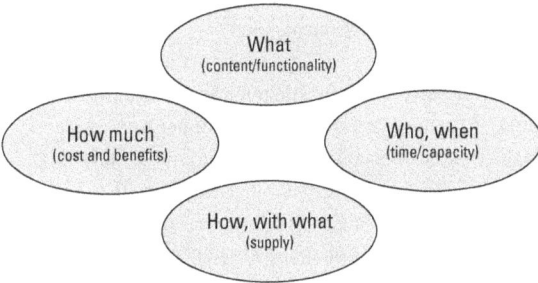

Figure 20 The subjects within the management process cluster

These four subjects can be found in the four processes within this cluster (see also Annex 5):

- *Planning and resource management* – deals with the subjects of time and staffing capacity necessary for managing information provisioning and carrying out changes to information provisioning.
- *Financial management* – deals with the costs and benefits of information provisioning and the associated investments.

- *Demand management* – covers the quality of information provisioning and information provisioning support, including the associated need for change or improvement.
- *Contract management* – regulates the control of IT providers, together with the agreements regarding services and products to be delivered.

The management of these processes deals integrally with the clusters *use management, functionality management* and the *connecting processes*. The *management processes* are also integral in another way: they look at the user organization, business information management, and IT.

Or, to be more specific: the costs do not just concern those of automated IT (such as for example, the price per work place) but also those of business information management and those associated with the use of information provisioning in the user organization. If, for example, a mobile phone enables the user to save half an hour a day, the final operational costs will be lower, while the IT costs increase.

6.2   Planning and resource management

Planning and resource management deals with the management of time and (human) capacity. This process therefore deals with the available time, necessary capacity, time needed, and delivery time. This concerns not only the capacity of the business information management function but also that of the IT providers, the user organization, and also the plans within the user organization.

The objectives behind *planning and resource management* are therefore:

- Making plans, and making time and capacity available in order to realize the services in the area of information provisioning, and any changes to this such as the necessary capacity for the *functionality management* and the *use management* clusters.
- Taking measures in order to produce extra capacity to satisfy the needs, or to take measures to reduce this capacity and to determine how to fulfill this question of capacity.
- Reducing or increasing the need for changes in information provisioning and coordinating this with the possibilities from the user organization, IT providers, and the business information management function.
- Monitoring the progress and effort associated with all this.

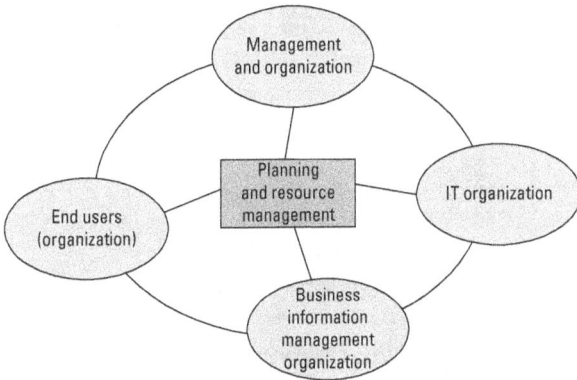

Figure 21 Planning and resource management

The *planning and resource management* process seems simpler than it is. This involves several parties such as one or several users departments and IT providers; it may often also include management.

The activities within the framework of *planning and resource management* are:

- Planning the time lines, reserving the staffing capacity (for the line work and 'project' changes) and coordinating the time lines over all parties (such as IT, business information management and user organization).
- Checking and monitoring capacity, availability, depletion, progress, and adjusting or taking measures as necessary.
- Evaluating the realization of the plans, recognizing or adjusting key figures and making suggestions for improvement.

From UPC practice
Planning and resource management was a process that was not actually carried out in the past. This recently caused more and more problems, also because there were 'some issues' and developments within UPC .

Before the re-structuring, the Board of Directors made considerable cuts in personnel in the supporting administrative departments (subscriptions and advertisements) with the result that these departments were left with much less time for activities outside the primary processes. Despite this, various new subscription forms have been introduced such as the weekend subscription and the Internet subscription, and the advertising department has also had to deal with more offers via the Internet, resulting in more pressure for those employees still in service.

This means business information management within the users' departments achieves considerably less and must come to an agreement with the departmental management much earlier if anyone wants anything.

This situation became patently obvious with the introduction of what was colloquially named as 'e-release'. The two new subscription forms, the weekend subscription and the Internet subscription were introduced in this release. At the same time, the commercial department started the end-of-year offensive, a campaign in which large-scale new and temporary subscriptions were sold on the late night shopping evenings, which produced still more work for the subscription department. And all this took place in December of all months when there is always extra pressure due to the several cancellations.

Business information management was also hard at work with the end-of-year processing (invoicing) and the preparation of the end-of-year accounts. Support for introducing the new release by business information management was minimal.

Despite all these events coinciding, coupled with the great amount of work pressure and stress within the departments, there were no major catastrophes. However, it was clear that it was actually unjustified, certainly for the employees in the subscription department, to have to do overtime on the various evenings just before Christmas. Patrick decided that it could happen once, but never again. It was clear that we had to get more of a grip on a number of things:

- insight into the desired changes for the coming year such
  as plans for mailings and new forms of products from
  marketing/commerce together with plans from the Board of
  Directors;
- insight into the use of in-house business information
  administrators. Some problems were also partly caused by
  business information management simply having too little
  time. Patrick realized that he did not have control of his
  own group at that particular time;
- insight into the workload within the user departments and
  the current capacity within the user organization to be able
  to carry out changes in information systems or methods.

Patrick also realized that the times when VGK issued releases
were extremely impractical. By chance, two delivery times
coincided with times when the user departments were under
maximum pressure.

Patrick's first step was to list the existing and planned
changes. He started with the change calendar, but also had
discussions with department heads, the Board of Directors,
and the commercial department. Patrick's second step
was to introduce a regular two-monthly consultation with
the management to discuss this calendar. For this, he also
reserved capacity for other smaller changes, so there was also
the possibility to address more urgent needs. And last but not
least, Patrick started with planning the capacity of business
information management.

This had direct effects. A recruitment campaign was delayed
by one month so enough room was left over for a new release.

As this was decided early enough, the commercial department had no problem with it. Patrick also realized that the capacity of the BIM group was insufficient. When he presented this problem to the Board of Directors, they came up with the great idea of having two BIM groups fuse quickly with those of Patrick. Of course this will not directly solve his problem: he will need a lot of time over the next three months to straighten everyone out and get everyone on side.

6.3   Financial management

Introduction
Financial management deals with managing and monitoring the costs and benefits of information provisioning and the changes in this. Central to this are therefore two terms, i.e., costs and benefits. These come together in the *business case*.

Costs
The costs include not only the expenses of automated information provisioning but also costs (or human resources) in the area of non-automated information provisioning. There are various types of costs, such as:
• The costs of automated information provisioning such as licenses, development and hardware, together with the costs for use the of software, management expenses, and maintenance costs.
• The costs of non-automated information provisioning such as forms, handbooks and supporting the business information management function.

- The costs of using information provisioning in the user process, and the efficiency of the use of information provisioning in the business process.
- One-off costs (the costs of changes) such as purchase costs, costs of automated and manual conversions, training costs.

Benefits

As well as costs, there are benefits such as increasing the productivity of the business processes. A business case does not just involve financial benefits. There are also other reasons to implement changes and only a few have clear demonstrable financial benefits. Other reasons can be:

- The satisfaction of users or clients or addressing sources of dissatisfaction.
- Obligations from the market or legislation ('It simply must be').
- The feeling that it simply must happen, that the policy is completed with this, or a direction is used ('I believe we must do this').
- Improvement of the starting point of the business process, information provisioning or automated information provisioning towards the future ('It improves our position').

There are, therefore, not just financial considerations and decision-making seldom takes place based purely on rational considerations and facts. The irrationality is also normally accepted within other subjects of operational management. An example by analogy: when buying a car, the purchase price alone is seldom the reason to purchase.

Options, comfortable seats, image and even personal considerations ('We always drive in a...') play an at least as important role in this. The same does actually apply to information provisioning.

The business case

Setting up the business case for information provisioning is the primary responsibility of business information management. The IT provider is regularly asked to set up such a business case, though they probably do not have the knowledge to do this. In order to be able to establish the benefits, you must know exactly how users now work, what it costs and what benefits a change produces.

The supplier also has another business case: the costs calculated are actually benefits for the supplier. These benefits are not always simply or clearly connected with the actual costs, certainly if there are shared infrastructures, systems or packages, and several clients. For the sake of clarity: it transpires that the financial management processes with BiSL and ITIL are

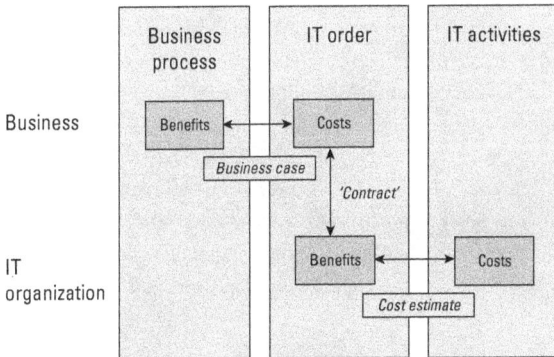

Figure 22 Cost and benefits depend on the perspective

designed from various perspectives, serve various interests, and
should therefore not be confused with one another.

From UPC practice

In the contract agreed by the Board of Directors, there was a
function specified that had an exorbitantly high price tag. It
was clear to Patrick, Robert and Lindsley that this function
would not be used, but the Board had already pushed for it
for reasons that were unclear. Patrick, Robert and Lindsley
then went to a café for a 'policy discussion': if the UPC Board
of Directors could throw away good money like that, so could
they!

The value and importance of PARIS, the advertising
system and all elements surrounding this are clear, which
is not always the case for the changes that UPC apply to
this. Lindsley also thought that something had to be done.
She has still not found a good system for quantifying any
benefits but with common sense, she will go far. The budget
monitoring was also always rather messed up. Two years
ago, the budget was used up, to everyone's surprise, by the
third quarter, whilst the previous year there was still a lot of
the budget unspent at the end of the year. Lindsley, as the
financial genius of business information management, was
to bring order into these things, and was given two priorities
by Patrick that she had also received from the Board of
Directors. She first had to ensure that a functional process
was created for budgeting and budget expenditure, whereby
key figures can be collected. The invoices were also controlled
more rigidly.

The second priority was that from now on, business cases were to be set up for larger changes. In these business cases, consideration must be made between costs, the benefits to the business process or other associated benefits, other reasons or arguments, and the ambition level of the solution. Lindsley created a template for this.

However, there are now other problems: VGK is going to increase the management costs. They have been busy with cost management in the context of profession-alization. This means that the real costs for management services to UPC are now known. The services to UPC are also changing. VGK therefore wishes to increase the management costs. The Board of Directors were not happy about this increase, though Lindsley is convinced that it is honest and realistic.

Patrick has also set a third priority himself: dealing in a structured way with benefits and developing a structured approach for mapping these out. However, this priority has been postponed. Lindsley has no idea how to approach it and, furthermore, she currently has another important focus of interest: there have been some urgent questions on PARIS and the rest of information provisioning from the finance department in relation to developments in the area of financial legislation.

6.4   Contract management

The *contract management* process deals with the consideration of setting up, monitoring and adjusting of the agreements and contracts in the area of information provisioning. In practice, this specifically covers contracts with the various IT functions/

providers. *Contract management* also fulfils the role of principal for the IT provider.

Contract management therefore has two areas of responsibility:
- Developing and agreeing the content of the contract and establishing effective relations with the supplier to ensure that they successfully meet the requirements of the contract.
- Monitoring the contract and the performance of the supplier and assessing the supplier, performance, and contract.

Pitfalls with contracts
One often tends to pay the most attention to the costs (rates) contained within contracts. Price is an important aspect but certainly not the only one. As information provisioning (information systems and technical infrastructure) are important for the business processes and the business processes are important for the organization, it follows that quality and reliability are important points of interest. Quality is generally at odds with costs. If one takes too much off the suppliers' margins, the solutions they offer are likely to be of lower quality. It is therefore important when considering or adjusting a contract to determine which characteristic is the most important at that point in time; price, reliability and quality, flexibility, or the level of innovation to name a few.

The contract also involves responsibilities. The fact that the supplier has responsibility for delivering the solution within an agreed budget means that they can decide how best to achieve this, which in turn means that the client no longer has control over the delivery method.

A third subject to address is the fact that demands change with time. Organizations go through various stages and phases over time (see Figure 23). The demands of information provisioning also change over time. Often, the reasons for setting up a contract change over a period of time. For example, whilst costs might have been the most important factor when the contract was originally set up, after say three years the most important issue might now be flexibility. This means setting up and agreeing another contract to reflect this. However, such updating of a contract is often forgotten.

A last pitfall that we should mention is the fact that one often tends to invest a lot of energy in defining and concluding formal contracts, only to then leave them untouched in the drawer without focusing on them.

Figure 23 Demands and phases of organizations (according to Hardjono)[2]

---

2 T.W. Hardjono, F.W. Hes, De Nederlandse kwaliteitsprijs en onderscheiding, Kluwer, Deventer 1993.

Management circle
Contract management and the contract itself start with
considering the content of the contract and the desired and/
or possible types of service. The following must be established:
the form that the services to be provided should take, which
conditions should apply, the management form and the supplier's
responsibilities, prices, and rates, etc.

This is seldom directly translated into a contract. Thoughts often
change during the contract negotiations or re-negotiations. After
concluding the contract, the contract will have to be monitored,
which means checking to see if the services are proceeding
according to the contract.

Continuous contact is also maintained with the supplier
regarding the process. Regular consideration must be given to
whether these services still fit in with the continually changing
business processes and whether the selected contract form,
the supplier, and the management form are consistent with the
desired situation. One must therefore assess whether the contract
and services still fit in with the needs of the organization. This
can lead to a new contract or re-negotiation.

Type of agreements
Agreements are often made with suppliers on various subjects
and in various documents. There may, for example, be framework
agreements (coordinating agreements on services), contracts
(agreements on specific services with prices and conditions),
SLAs (measurable and operational agreements on how the
services are performing), agreements about how cooperation will
take place and how the organization is operationally designed as
well as preferred supplier agreements.

From UPC practice

Contract management was forced upon UPC by VGK as
the UPC Board of Directors had a dispute with VGK. The
UPC Board had demanded that VGK should start working
according to agreed contractual terms and VGK subsequently
submitted a contract based on this. The Board of Directors
thought the price was too high, requested a 20% discount,
and then signed the contract.

Just before going on holiday, the new contract appeared on
Patrick's desk stating that the Board of Directors assumed
that the contract would be managed and monitored by
Business information management. Patrick delegated this role
to Robert and appointed him as contract manager. It took
Robert six months to discover that the contract was not ideal.
The contract included service levels prepared by an external
consultant tasked by the UPC Board of Directors together
with VGK.

With this contract and the service levels, UPC had assumed
responsibility for processing various system functions: VGK
had passed back the responsibility for these tasks to UPC
as 20% of the costs had to be saved. There were also the
necessary interfaces, reports, and forms that had to be signed
each time, and the contract was hardly flexible.

Urgent processing must be requested one month in advance.
This does not, however, always fit in with the sometimes
slightly chaotic way of working at UPC.

Both VGK and UPC now agreed that this contract was far from ideal. Also Bert who is responsible for the *operational supplier management* process and had the thankless task of digging through the enormous volume of service level reports had already complained to Robert. Fortunately, the latter had immediately been able to agree to a somewhat different work method in practice.

Together with Patrick, he went looking for other contracts with suppliers that may be more suitable. As part of this exercise they stumbled on a contract for an advertising system that has not been used for one-and-a-half years, but for which payments were still made. In consultation with the Board of Directors, it was decided to carry out a business-wide inventory of IT contracts.

Robert had also been in continuous discussion with VGK regarding the current contract and both parties noted the points they would like to see changed. Both UPC and VGK have further-reaching interests: both hope that the contract can be a model for contracts with other suppliers (for UPC) and other clients (for VGK). It is also clear for Robert that the demands of UPC means that flexibility and reliability have become much more important than costs. This has resulted in the first move for a new contract. Both VGK and UPC are very satisfied with this. Now, only the Board of Directors has to be convinced and the contract can be signed.

6.5 Demand management

Objective
The objective of the *demand management* process is to guarantee
the information provisioning fits in with the business process
on a management level for example, if there are new products,
new legislation, or a growing number of users. Central to this
is the quality of information provisioning (and mainly the
shortcomings or the needs for change) and the changes that result
from alterations in the business processes or the environment
surrounding this information provisioning and which must be
carried out in the short- and medium term.

This quality consists of:
- quality of the information provisioning
- quality of the services and quality of the processing of the
  services.

Quality of the information provisioning
The quality of the information provisioning is intrinsic in nature:
by this, we mean that it refers to information provisioning
(information systems and technical infrastructure) in relation
to the business processes. This, therefore, concerns how the
functions of information provisioning fit in with the business
processes, user organization, and users.

This therefore concerns subjects as:
- Fitting in with the business process and information
  provisioning – the extent to which the business process and
  the steps in the business process fit in with the steps in the
  information provisioning and the functions of the information
  system. Think of steps such as entering a request for a

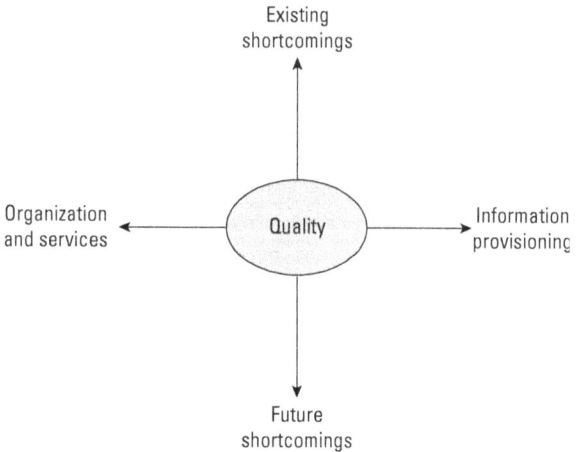

Figure 24 The axes of quality and demand

quotation, processing offers, offer acceptance, feedback to intermediaries, etc.

- Ergonomics – the extent to which information provisioning fits in with the knowledge and skills of the users and the extent to which they can deal efficiently and effectively with information provisioning.
- Information quality – the extent to which information provisioning provides information and information requirements, for example, for management or carrying out the business process.

Needs may be twofold by nature:

- There is a gap: information provisioning is of insufficient quality to support the current situation (and a change is therefore required).

- A gap occurs if nothing is done. This involves developments that will play a part in coming years and make changes in information provisioning necessary. Examples of this include changes to legislation, new products, other methods of management and competition.

Quality of the services
Quality can also refer to the process of services and support to information provisioning by the various functions in the area of information provisioning. These are the functions in the following areas: business information management, IT infrastructure management and/or application management. Also here, there may be existing shortcomings together with the changing needs of the organization. Think for example of longer opening times (for example the requirement for the availability of information provisioning in the evening hours), dealing with incidents quicker, increased reliability of the specifications and the delivered products, a greater degree of security of information provisioning, etc.

From UPC practice
It was always difficult for the UPC business information administrators to look far ahead. Change requests would often arrive at the last minute. This meant, for example, that consistency between the Internet-based information and the advertising system only became clear when the new website was launched on the Internet. It was an initiative of the marketing department and they forgot to inform the relevant people. There were also quite a few complaints about the information systems particularly regarding the debtor module without this resulting in any change requests.

Lindsley thought these were all incentives to now carry out
a structured approach towards *demand management* and
follow the needs and developments in- and outside UPC more
proactively. They started undertaking a quality inventory
of the advertising- and subscription system in order to map
out how well these fitted in with the business processes. This
revealed various interesting points, small and large, that were
interesting enough to do something about. It turned out that
the staff in accounts receivable, most of whom were from the
former PC, were very annoyed at the terminology used within
UP and which also appeared on most screens within the
financial module.

And there were three virtually identical reports distributed
via PARIS that have still not been used at all.

Lindsley also discovered that almost four out of ten end
users still had not heard of the new business information
management department. That was a shocking discovery for
Patrick and led directly to new *end user support* guidelines.
In any case, this all seemed sufficient grounds for setting up
a need calendar. The existing change requests and the non-
formalized needs are entered into this. Some of these have
also been entered in the VGK change calendar in consultation
with VGK.

The inventory also went to corporate information management but this did not lead to anything. PARIS and the other
systems have no place in the vision of corporate information
management bearing in mind these are not based on a SOAP
architecture. Lindsley has her doubts over the validity of

this argument but she is unconcerned. Finally, the business information management department itself has a budget and therefore does not really need anything from corporate information management.

7 Information strategy cluster

7.1 Introduction

The previous chapter dealt with the *management processes*.
Management demands a long-term vision, a direction one
must aim for. This vision is developed in three process clusters:
information strategy cluster, *I-organization strategy* cluster,
and *information coordination*. In the following chapters, these
clusters of the strategic level will be described in a slightly more
concise format than the previous process clusters. We begin with
the *information strategy* cluster.

Within the *information strategy* cluster the vision on the future
of information provisioning is made. It describes what shape
information provisioning (information processes, information
systems, and any technology) will take over three to five
years. This cluster deals with the content of the information
provisioning and not how this is organized. This end product is
often also called an information policy.

Basic points
Before we go into the description of the processes, we shall
consider a number of observations and views.

- *Information provisioning changes but less than one thinks.*
  The existing situation is generally a good starting point.

An organization is seldom stable, the business processes are
however to a great extent. The (desired) functionality of an

information provisioning system is therefore often more stable
than one thinks.

The business processes of banks, insurance companies,
government and other organizations experience over a long
period a high degree of stability in terms of how they are carried
out. Parameters however change, including the necessary
management parameters but the essential processes remains
similar. Almost everything is automated that an organization
can automate. This is also evident from the average lifetime of
information provisioning systems, which is over ten years. This
means there is no longer a demand for automation but a demand
for replacement. Over a five year-period, we will probably still
see a requirement for 80% of the functionality of information
provisioning. This gives rise to the question of whether
everything must be designed and built again from scratch.

There are of course changes and the effectiveness with which one
approaches and translates these needs will determine the quality
of information provisioning over five years. It is therefore often
a good idea to start with determining how good information
provisioning is now, what specific change demands there are
and what impact the organization's new policy will have on
information provisioning. By mapping out these specific change
demands, one also gains a specific picture of the possible solution
directions.

- *It is difficult to develop a policy with a horizon of seven years.
  Striving to achieve a competitive position over three years is
  often more effective.*

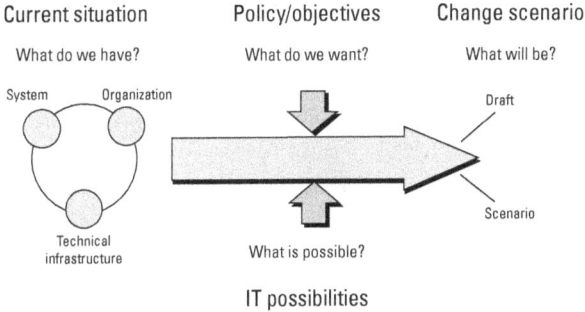

Current situation
What do we have?

System   Organization

Technical infrastructure

Policy/objectives
What do we want?

What is possible?

IT possibilities

Change scenario
What will be?

Draft

Scenario

Figure 25 Aspects of renewal

For large organizations, the realization time for far-reaching changes in information provisioning will have a lead time (including conceptualization and decision-making) of between three to seven years. This makes it very difficult to create information policy: who can estimate how an organization and the world will look like seven years hence and what will be important then? Considering trends such as transfers, fusions, outsourcing, globalization, centralization or decentralization, means that it is difficult to have a set picture over such a long period.

It is often, therefore, a more sensible approach not to strive for the perfect information provisioning over five or seven years (for example, by re-designing everything) but rather to ensure that the basic situation in the area of information provisioning over three years is good and that one can follow the desired developments in an acceptable manner. In other words: it is often a better idea to make the existing information provisioning as competitive as possible over three years instead of striving for perfect information provisioning in the long term. Finally, an organization competes in the marketplace with its existing information provisioning and not with information provisioning that one has five years time, as the current information provisioning determines the strength of the competition.

- *Information strategy is created on a minimum of two levels: the policy regarding the entire concept and the policy regarding the parts of this.*

First, there is the level of the entire information provisioning of an organization. This involves coherence, standards, and assessment of the various parts of information provisioning. Policy is however also made regarding part of information provisioning. A policy will, for example, also be made regarding the future of the (existing) information provisioning for the domain of personnel information provisioning or non-life insurance. This policy is seldom a derivative of the coordinating policy and there are various reasons for this.

Non-life insurance and personnel information provisioning often act independently of one another, are often based on a different situation, and also have different stakeholders.

The policy on the corporate level and the underlying level are therefore not automatically extensions of one another: it must therefore be coordinated.

The processes within the cluster
The *information strategy* cluster involves five processes of which three are inventoried and two are policy-forming, see also Annex 5.

There are developments coming from three sides that can lead to structural change to an organization's information provisioning:

- Within the user organization and the business processes, a range of changes occur as a result of changes in policy or forced by the environment.
- There are developments in technology such as suppliers who stop supporting technology with the result that the existing applications can no longer be used, or new technology comes onto the market that offers the possibility of new ways of working.
- The information provisioning forms part of an information chain in which changes take place.

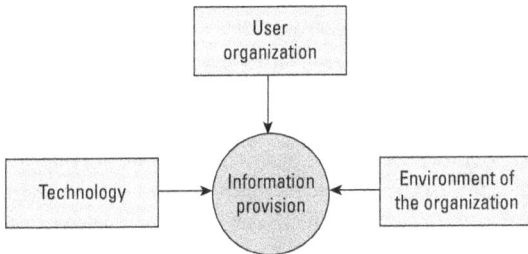

Figure 26 Developments that influence information provisioning

The inventorying processes have more or less already been introduced by stating the places where developments can come from:

- Business process and user organization *(establish business process developments)*
- Technology *(establish technological developments)*
- Environment *(establish information chain developments)*.

There are also two policy-forming processes central within this cluster. These are a result of the already mentioned starting point of policy on two levels:

- *Information lifecycle management* in which policy is formed for an information domain.
- *Information portfolio management* in which the policy is formed and the coordination is realized over the entire information provisioning.

7.2   Establish information chain developments

Organizations communicate more and more with one another partly through the possibilities offered by IT. Businesses processes from various organizations are connected with one another more and more through networks and (automated) data exchange, whilst the dependencies between organizations are considerably increased by this. The functioning of these communications and alterations in these exchanges directly affect an organization's business process and image. For example, a mistake in the data or data processing is directly visible for the outside world. Cooperation with other independent organizations with whom there is no business trading partnership is seldom compelling. This means the carrying out of changes is a phase demanding considerably more time and consideration. The objective of *establish information chain developments* is listing the changes and the possibilities that chain automation offers the business process and information provisioning.

7.3   Establish business process developments

It is not only organizations, but also relatively stable business processes that change continuously as a result of developments in the outside world. These developments also lead to changes in information provisioning.

There are two types of developments and the impact is often
varied:

- Developments in the business process – most changes in the
  business process such as a new policy, a more flexible product,
  another link or report to clients, new rules, or legal provisions
  are implemented quite gradually. These changes are often
  part of a creeping fundamental development whereby the
  demands on information provisioning and the desired set-up
  of this will change more or less invisibly over time.
- Developments in the organization and the control – this
  type of change such as de-centralization, centralization, cost
  consciousness or quality awareness are quite revolutionary
  (it happens at a certain time) and are highly visible for both
  organization and management. These are normally less far-
  reaching for information provisioning of the primary business
  process.

The objective of *establish business process development* is listing
which developments and changes occur, have occurred, or will
occur so that the influence of this on information provisioning
can be determined and the set up and completion of information
provisioning can be adjusted to reflect this.

7.4 Establish technological developments

Developments in technology also impact on information
provisioning. Developments in technology enable new
possibilities to arise for supporting the business processes
(such as accessing the client information system on location
via a browser). It may also be that certain possibilities become
affordable or interesting (such as a standard package that could
change customized services). Existing used technology can also
become outdated and no longer supported so the organization
must reserve significant means to migrate the existing solutions or

procure alternative solutions. The process *establish technological developments* maps out these types of developments and trends. The technology to which we refer is not just specific hardware technology such as computers and networks but also the software. The result of this process is opportunities and threat from the developments in the technology.

7.5   Information lifecycle management

The first central process within the cluster is *information lifecycle management*. This process can be summarized as determining the policy on an information domain, for example, the personnel information system. In this, one illustrates the shape that information provisioning on a domain should take after three to seven years and which scenarios there are for achieving this.

It is also desirable for decision-making to take place based on specific information. This information will for example, refer to:
• The technical quality and exploitation quality – the quality and maintainability of the technical information system or what possibilities one now has for technical information provisioning.
• The functional quality – the extent to which the information system fits in with the business process and the users.
• The developments in the technology and the environment of the organization.
• The policy of the organization, the changes this involves for current information provisioning, and the influence of this on information provisioning.

Based on this information, one makes judgements on the competitiveness and the ability to future-proof information provisioning, and also on the necessity of phasing out, renovating,

re-constructing, or structurally improving the associated IT.
One also formulates the shape that information provisioning
is to take and which scenarios will be chosen. The decision-
making depends largely on the possibilities and the scope the
organization has to change. This often also leads to adjustment of
the ambitions, the proposed policy of the organization, and also
the scenarios one is to follow, such as:

- Carrying out the changes within the regular process of
  management and maintenance.
- Reconstructing, constructing afresh, or purchasing a new
  technical information provisioning ('information system').
- Structural renewal or upgrading of existing information
  provisioning.
- Standardization of the business processes and information
  provisioning used for this.

7.6   Information portfolio management

Information lifecycle management deals with the design and
completion of the parts in information provisioning (such
as the personnel information provisioning and the damage
systems). Coordinating this also requires a policy and a vision.
The *information portfolio management* process deals with
determining or coordinating the policy regarding the entire
information provisioning and the monitoring of the coherence
of information provisioning of an organization or organizations.
The importance behind this is twofold:

- The feasibility of all developments and changes within
  information provisioning in the organization. Or the question:
  can the organization manage all this and are dependencies
  between changes covered.
- The collectivity and coherence of information provisioning
  within the entire organization. The various information

domains (such as personnel information provisioning) are
related and the coherence of all of this is also an important
point of interest.

The subject of *information portfolio management* is therefore
the information provisioning of the entire organization and the
coherence therein.

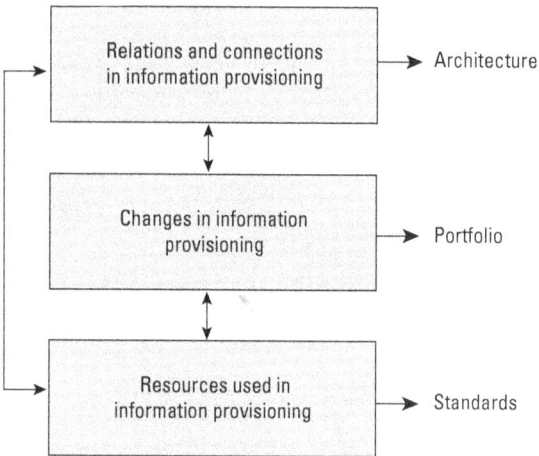

Figure 27 The subjects within information portfolio management

This means there are three central subjects within the
information portfolio management process:
- Standards operated in an organization for information
  provisioning. Standards enable economies of scale throughout
  the organization and often lead to an improvement in the
  compatibility of parts.
- Architecture of the information provisioning – the build up of
  information provisioning in sub-domains. providing clarity in

the relations and coherence with these parts. This therefore also includes recognizing the limits of these domains.
- Portfolio of fundamental changes to the organization. The various (more far-reaching) changes must be mutually agreed and mutually prioritized if necessary.

In order to be able to make these assessments, one must compare the various attributes of the information portfolio such as the technical and functional condition of the parts of information provisioning and the importance, the impact, and the priority of the various developments in information provisioning. The possible solution directions with the extent, impact, and time lines will also be considered in their entirety in an organization as well as any introduction of new technological possibilities. This means that one receives a portfolio such as displayed in Figure 28.

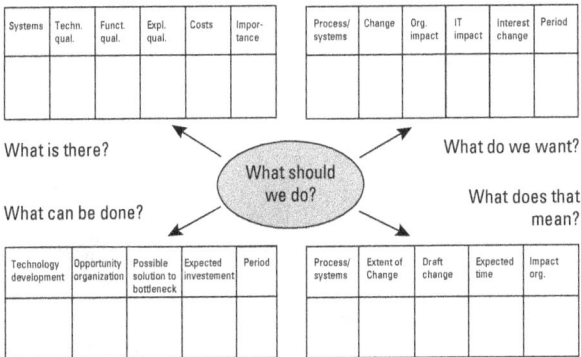

Systems	Techn. qual.	Funct. qual.	Expl. qual.	Costs	Impor- tance

Process/ systems	Change	Org. impact	IT impact	Interest change	Period

What is there?

What do we want?

What should we do?

What can be done?

What does that mean?

Technology development	Opportunity organization	Possible solution to bottleneck	Expected investement	Period

Process/ systems	Extent of Change	Draft change	Expected time	Impact org.

Figure 28 The attributes of the information portfolio

From UPC practice

Patrick has started, together with his group, to approach the *information lifecycle management* process in a more structured manner. The *management processes* are now in reasonable condition and there is the opportunity of looking more into the future. The developments concerning the Internet also require this more and more.

Two years ago, a session was held to discuss the expectations and wishes of UPC with regards to PARIS over the coming three year period. A consultant was hired to supervise the process. Patrick already thought it was a better idea to do so for the entire information provisioning of the BIM group but there was not really time for this at that point.

In any case, the session resulted in a suggestion for a new system, My-Subscription, with which subscribers could themselves quickly get information and adjust their subscription details. This new system is now scheduled for implementation half-way through next year and reactions to the advertisements with the strap line, 'Quickly a paper, quickly no paper' are very positive.

During this session, a photo was used from the BiSL book (complemented with other books) and that produced enough handles to deal with the process. It also led to a report that could be used as a template for a subsequent session. The process was also seen as a success, providing excellent service as best practice for the next time. Hard data and information on the information provisioning were available, while time was also left over for irrational arguments and information.

The management had assisted in this session, which pleased Patrick a great deal. He gained the impression that the Board of Directors understood everything that was at stake and which issues, both straightforward and complex, Patrick was dealing with. The Board also seemed to understand how dependent UPC is from information provisioning.

From the feedback, it turned out that the Board of Directors was also very satisfied. For the first time they received an insight into and understanding of information provisioning. No fancy stories, just concrete information, in a way that was understood by all.

The Board now understood that certain demands were very extensive and that the costs in some cases were not in direct relation to the benefits. They also realized that they could manage the costs of information provisioning themselves and realistic and sensible decision-making over this was possible.

It was also understood that UPC's competitive position depended to a degree on what was possible now with information provisioning and that there had been little consideration of this in previous years.

Because the results were pragmatic and realistic, it was fairly easy to take these forward and turn them into practice. And so 'My Subscription" is now in the pipeline.

8 I-organization strategy cluster

8.1 Introduction

Several organizations are generally involved in information provisioning. In practice, there are quite a few differences of opinion regarding activities, responsibilities, roles, and interest. One of the most important reasons as to why there are many disputes in organizations regarding information provisioning is that the interests and responsibilities for information provisioning are not acknowledged or recognized, they have not been established, or are themselves conflicting. It is therefore important to:

- Make agreements on cooperation between persons/functions in the area of information provisioning.
- Have clarity regarding the mandates and responsibilities and coordinate these with the interests.
- Streamline the processes with which information and decision-making take place.

The objective of the *I-organization strategy* cluster is to set up and adjust the organization of information provisioning and determine the strategy as to how to achieve this.

Processes
There are various people or parties within and external to an organization that have a say, an opinion, or must be listened to regarding information provisioning. We distinguish between four types:

- User departments (management)
- Suppliers

- (Other) business information management organizations
- Chain partners

This cluster therefore recognizes four processes, each geared to the type of target group. The processes are (see also Annex 5):
- *Strategic supplier management*
- *Strategic information partner management*
- *Strategic user relationship management*
- *Define I-organization strategy*

Figure 29 Processes within the I-organization strategy cluster

8.2   Strategic supplier management

The role of suppliers within information provisioning is changing. There are a few developments underway whereby suppliers in the area of information provisioning will be assigned other more significant roles:
- IT functions assume responsibilities as a result of the commercialization of the relations between clients and IT function, and due to IT functions (organizations) operating

in a more result-oriented manner. The IT function (supplier) is therefore being given more say over the solution and the process of realization. This means that business information management has less to manage on the technical content.

- The market for standard solutions is also growing. Standard solutions such as package- or ASP solutions (whereby the supplier offers ready-made functionality, the necessary technical infrastructure behind this, and the processing function) lead to the situation where the supplier primarily decides on the functionality himself. So, once again, the level of involvement is less for business information management. One can for example, no longer decide oneself as to which functionality the solution must provide.
- Suppliers are becoming specialized as IT solutions become more complex, meaning the possibility of managing the supplier is more difficult and the importance of choosing the right supplier over the right solution is greater.
- The dependence of business processes upon IT solutions is growing and, as a consequence, so is the importance of selecting the right supplier.

Strategic supplier management is therefore becoming more important. An organization will ask itself more questions and formulate the answers to these, for example:

- Which suppliers are there, what range of services do these suppliers offer, which suppliers are good in offering specific services and specific technology, and which suppliers are capable of fulfilling a role in terms of the organization's information provisioning?
- What behavior is desirable from the various suppliers, what are the expectations and what is the relationship between the

results and these expectations? What are the relations with a supplier?

- How shall we select a supplier? What form does supplier selection take?
- What is the dependence of the organization regarding a supplier, what is the organization's position on this and what is the relationship between this and the supplier's ability to continue in business?
- Which responsibilities must one give the supplier? What framework agreements are there or should there be?

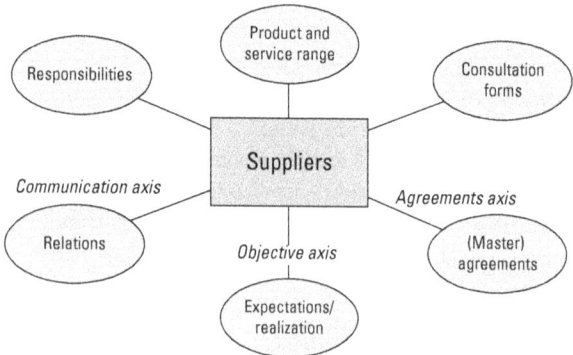

Figure 30 Subjects within strategic supplier management

Determining the policy regarding these questions forms the key to *strategic supplier management*. There are three parts (sub-processes) within *strategic supplier management*:

- Supplier policy – the formulating of policy over how to deal with suppliers in general and specific suppliers in particular.
- Supplier selection and assessment – determining of answers to questions such as: how do suppliers perform currently and which suppliers will be selected for which parts of IT services?

- Supplier management – the organization, management and exchange of information on the relations that exist with a specific supplier at various levels within the organization.

8.3   Strategic information partner management

Organizations work together with other organizations and receive information from other organizations. Chain partners are organizations with whom information is exchanged. Other than for example, an internal organizational department with whom information is exchanged, in principle chain partners cannot be managed. They are not part of the organization, they have their own management and Board of Directors. Therefore, the power to actually manage these chain partners is lacking.

In setting up or changing information exchange chains, clear agreements must be made in advance as to the importance of every party in this information chain and what contributions are made. Dealing with chain partners therefore demands another approach. In most cases, agreements must be made earlier and also on a higher level. More consideration will also be paid in advance as to the method (desired or undesired) by which changes in the information provisioning are carried out and what is to be done if incidents or problems occur.

The process of *strategic information partner management* therefore deals with making agreements with the various members of a chain over the method of cooperation, which agreements and responsibilities there are, what contributions are made by the various organizations in this chain, and how changes are dealt with.

8.4   Strategic user relationship management

The third process relates to the user organization itself, of which business information management is a part. Ideally, business information management is the portfolio holder of 'information provisioning' for the user organization, or a part of this. In addition, the management of the user organization is responsible for information provisioning.

Agreements are therefore necessary between business information management and the user organization and the relations between them must be developed. It is important that all levels within the user organization be covered from the domain business information management. Business information management organizations are regularly represented on the operational but not on the strategic level, or the other way round.

Strategic user relationship management ensures that the structure and management relations within the user organization are coordinated with the function within business information management and that business information management also has good relations with the various levels within the user organization so that all relevant information on use, developments, and plans are included in the decision-making on information provisioning.

Three subjects are central to this:
- Mandate – what mandate does business information management have from the user organization in order to make decisions regarding information provisioning, to what level does business information management decide directly, and from what level is this agreed with management.

- Communication – how is communication organized at
  the various levels within the user organization and which
  committees and consultation forms does one have.
- Approach – how does one approach the user organization
  from the business information management function and what
  is the position (serving, facilitating, coordinating, etc.).

The last point demands some explanation. Lines of power
within the user organization(s) determine the lines of power of
business information management. In a highly de-centralized
organization, a business information management organization
cannot operate in a highly centralized manner. In such a
situation a central business information management will have to
operate in a supporting, facilitating, coordinating, or enquiring
manner if one does want to have problems in the long term. In a
centralized organization, business information management can,
on instructions from management, act in a much more guiding
manner towards the underlying user departments.

8.5   Define I-organization strategy

The last process deals with relations within all management
functions in the area of the information provisioning (in other
words, the entire business information management domain).

Certainly within larger organizations there is seldom *one*
business information management function. There are sometimes
various BIM groups operating at various locations within the
organization, each with its own information domain (personnel,
logistics, etc.). Next to these BIM groups there is sometimes also
a coordinating business information management function (an
umbrella form of business information management) or there
is a separate policy function for information management. This

breakdown is a logical result of the structure, management, and coherence of the user organization; it is therefore almost always practical or effective.

There are therefore normally several locations where the information provisioning is managed and policies made. These parts seldom work well together: people sometimes dispute other people's powers or methods, or information is not exchanged as people do not know each other, or because there is a lack of understanding of how relevant this information is. *Define I-organization strategy* deals with coordinating the structure, the powers, the coherence, and the methods of these various business information management functions.

The *define I-organization strategy* process therefore complements the:
- Structure, set-up and possible coherence of the organization(s) in the area of business information management.
- Responsibilities and mandates of this (these) organization(s).
- Methods by which the communication and coordination has been arranged internally in these organization(s).
- Processes and methods with which one works.

Within this process, there are three sub-processes or activities:
- Assessing the situation regarding the above-mentioned subjects.
- Based on this, policy is formulated and actions are implemented for change or improvement.
- Management or adjustment is carried out if the structure is not satisfactory, or if the rules are not complied with, or in the case of conflict.

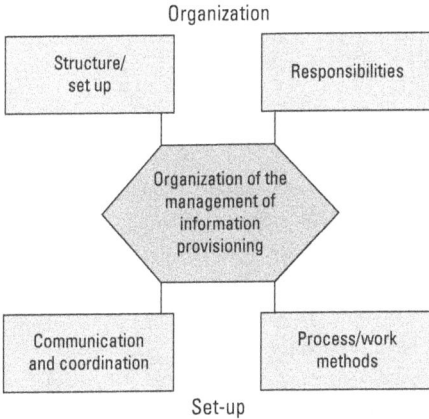

Figure 31 Subjects within define I-organization strategy

From UPC practice

Patrick is very satisfied with the changes over recent years within business information management. Everything is still far from being perfect but many milestones have been achieved at the operational and management levels. Last year, Patrick and his team met to discuss the experiences of Lindsley who found out that there were still users who did not know the department. They took a structured look at the user organization as well as the relations and the contacts they had.

The relations with Patrick's bosses have also been examined. A few improvement campaigns have been identified including formalization of the consultation forms. Relations with the supplier were also dealt with on that day. Patrick and Robert then entered into discussions with VGK in order to achieve new completion of the services, whereby VGK was to assume more responsibility.

All of this led to a dispute within UPC. CIM, the UPC Corporate Information Management department makes policies and has set up framework agreements with the most important suppliers including VGK but these did not fit in with Patrick's view of things. CIM also sets information strategy but little or nothing is done with this. Two years ago, CIM determined that all systems must work according to a SOAP architecture and that interfacing via XML must take place. Nothing has been done about this. No separate budget has been released for the necessary adjustments as everything must come from the regular (line) budgets and these are needed for the necessary extension of the existing system functionality. Also, the new MySubscription system finally fulfils requirements, but does that poorly in the view of CIM.

CIM had complained about this several times to the Board of Directors during the past year and had escalated the situation at a certain point. Fortunately, Patrick's bosses were completely behind Patrick in the subsequent conflict and went totally against CIM. To his surprise, they also received the support of the Board of Directors in this. The latter had a positive feeling in previous years as regards Patrick's BIM group. Also the extraordinarily positive experiences from the workshops regarding the future of information provisioning in the framework of lifecycle management had contributed to this.

The results of this conflict were, therefore, totally different from what CIM had expected and hoped for in advance. The Board of Directors drew the conclusion that CIM was too technological and too detached and was sitting in an ivory tower meaning that it could not operate effectively. The Board of Directors has now stipulated that the management and organization must be done differently.

And so the steps achieved with business information management in Patrick's department must be extended to the rest of the business. CIM may meanwhile define what its new role is without the costs being borne by the BIM groups. The various BIM groups now come to the table regularly in order share their knowledge and experiences with one another. Patrick knows that his department has a lot to offer here but was also impressed by the knowledge and experience of the other departments during the first meeting. They will certainly learn a lot from one another in the future.

The groups are also entering into talks with CIM and the various responsibilities will be determined in consultation. The BIM groups have stated their need for the spreading of information relating to suppliers, supplier selection, and exchange with chain partners. Now, there is also a recognition of the need to consider, throughout the group, links to client information that is held in various points throughout the business.

Patrick has achieved a great feeling despite, or perhaps even because of, these adventures. He has seen the Board of Directors and the management become increasingly impressed with the results achieved slowly by himself and his group. It is also clear that they have gained confidence in this. 'And I get a great kick out of it', he told Robert and Lindsley in confidence.

9 Information coordination

9.1 Introduction

The previous chapter dealt with the organization of the various parties in the wide area of information provisioning and the associated policy. The chapter before that dealt with the intrinsic policy on information provisioning and the parts of this. There are relations between these various forms of policy. The policy is, however, formulated from various angles. This leads to the need for communication and coordination. This is illustrated in the following example.

Complexity

An example of the complexity can be found in the table in Figure 32. An organization has six relatively independent information domains with various management structures and users. One recognizes, for example, a domain technical infrastructure (including work places, Internet/intranet and networks) that comes under the control of the Management resources. The policy and business information management are carried out by CIM (corporate information management). Suppliers in this area are Getrade, EBM and a few others. There is also a domain for logistical and financial information provisioning under the overall responsibility of Finance management. The business information management activities are carried out by the BIM group staff and resources. Getrade acts as supplier here but Map Sagitta and Logic are also important suppliers.

Dependencies

As a suppliers' policy is formulated for the supplier Getrade, this has an impact for the information domains Logistical information, SME & private persons, and Technical infrastructure. A policy regarding chain partner e-net has an impact on the information domains SME & private persons, the Business market, and Logistical information.

If the SME & private persons unit decides on far-reaching changes to the information provisioning in this area, this will have an impact on both the chain partners e-net and PayInternational, and also for the supplier Getrade among others.

	Logistical information	Financial information provisioning	Personnel information provisioning	information provisioning SME & private	Information provisioning business market	Infrastructure
User departments						
Finance Management	X	X				
P&O Management			X			
SME and private unit	X			X		
Business market unit	X				X	
Management resources						X
Suppliers						
Getrade	X			X		X
Logic		X				
Map Sagitta	X				X	
EBM			X			X
EPS				X		
Others		X	X			X
Chain partners						
E-net	X			X	X	
PayInternational		X		X	X	
E-forum NI	X					
Bim and IM organizations						
bim resources and staff information provisioning	X	X	X			
bim private				X		
bim business					X	
CIM						X

Figure 32 The complex relations between suppliers, information domains, and users

It is clear that, in most organizations, a Financial Director will not wish to forego the control over the area of financial information provisioning, just as the director for SMEs & private persons would not want this for his information provisioning. There is also a desire to have a transparent policy regarding suppliers. This shows that all these various forms of policy have consequences for other areas. It is also difficult to clearly design this form of policy from one place, managed *top down*. Harmony and coordination are therefore necessary between all these plans and policy forms.

These needs are met by *information coordination*. The objective of *information coordination* is monitoring and supervising the coherence of the plans for information provisioning and the information provisioning organizations.

This work therefore mainly involves communicating and coordinating: communicating the various plans to the different parties involved and having the developments communicated to one another. It is often a good idea not to operate in a completing and designing manner but in a coordinating and harmonizing manner, as a kind of umpire or process supervisor: allow the various parties involved to speak to one another and intervene when there are discrepancies that are outside of the agreements that have been made.

From UPC practice
Patrick never really managed to read the last chapter of BiSL, and he also has some difficulty in gaining an insight into what *information coordination* precisely means. For the time being

he has a few problems, bearing in mind that things at a guiding level are still not really regulated very well.

He spoke about this once at a birthday party with Brigitte, a niece of his, who works in the area of *information coordination*. He later made an appointment with her and she explained it all to him. Brigitte is an information manager at the DPG bank, which is a very large bank. At the bank, there are various people and departments responsible for various areas. There are supplier managers, for example, for BTOS, Getrade, Logic, who formulate the policies in these areas. There are also information managers who make policies for information provisioning in the area of bank processes, counter- and online banking, insurance, and other areas. There are roles for people managing the relations with various chain partners such as Interpay. All these policies have several relations with one another, something that one could not understand in the past.

And it cost quite a lot of money. For example, when a supplier manager entered into commercial commitments regarding the services of Logic without involving the respective information managers in this. These information managers had other plans, which meant that the commitments could not be fulfilled. As a result it was necessary to surrender the contract. And a few other similar problems arose. It had become clear at the DPG bank that all of these policies had to be coordinated and that this had to be organized.

Brigitte must now ensure that policy in one area is coordinated to policies in the other areas and that all these developments are coordinated. It is also her responsibility to ensure that this is still the case following continual changes in the organization. She has told Patrick that she finds it an extraordinarily exciting job. She sometimes feels like a process supervisor and sometimes an umpire but it's not easy.

Patrick has understood from these stories that these problems mainly occur when the organization is set up on the level of the guiding processes and the various roles have been designated. UPC is still not ready for this. He has nevertheless asked Brigitte to give a presentation in the autumn for the UPC management. And the subject of business information management and BiSL will be back on the agenda and that's never a bad idea.

10 Starting with business information management and BiSL

How can one best start with business information management and BiSL? There are various sources and instruments to help you on your way. A good starting point is the website of the ASL BiSL Foundation (www.aslbislfoundation.org). Here, you will find links to a BiSL self-assessment, education on BiSL, and of course, the *best practices* that are brought together by the partners of the ASL BiSL Foundation. This website also contains articles and white papers on how to implement and organize business information management. Also some books give consideration to this (Annex 4).

We can give you the following tips:
- Many process implementations went wrong in the past by working in a way that attempted to be too perfect and was too dogmatic, too theoretical, or too instrumental. Pragmatism is a great virtue in most situations.
- Mainly in the cases of business information management – but certainly not only in this case – an organization operates in a context that does not possess ideal preconditions. A business information management organization must often cooperate with other business information management groups, or even experience opposition from other groups of internal or external policy makers. The pure theory is therefore largely contaminated by everyday practice.

- Business information management is often in a situation that is primarily managed by the supplier in terms of the functionality in relation to information provisioning, for example, when use is made of packages. In such a situation, one must therefore organize processes from that perspective.
- The starting point of the existing business information management can differ considerably in experience, history, culture, and knowledge. Each set-up of business information management is therefore custom-made.

You must think carefully before starting. You must determine the ambition level, consider what the costs could be or make inquiries about this, determine what you have left over, establish what you wish to achieve, how urgent this is, when you wish to achieve this, and how feasible this is. However, almost this entire book deals with this sort of question.

ANNEX 1
The UPC case

This book features a company called UPC, which stands
for United Publishing Combination. In order to gain a
good understanding of the situation regarding information
provisioning in this company, we provide a report on recent
developments with which the company has been involved.

History
UPC is the result of the merger of several publishers. The
organization was created twelve years ago through the merger
of United Publishers and the Publishing Combination. This
combination has taken over various other publishers over the
last ten years and for some time has been the largest publisher in
England in the area of newspapers and magazines.

The automation is largely outsourced to VGK. This organization,
UPC's former IT department, became privatized by UPC five
years ago. This meant that VGK also had the possibility to
access the market outside UPC, something that succeeded well
with the help of partners. This privatization also gave UPC the
possibility of hiring other IT organizations and provided more
competitiveness in the area of IT. This privatization therefore
meant the beginning of a commercialization and a more
businesslike management of information provisioning and IT
within UPC.

The restructuring of UPC
Some time ago, UPC began restructuring its work. The underlying publishers were previously self-employed and the labels

with which UPC approached the outside world were mainly the names of their publishers such as Nolters, Meestrichter, and NDU. By the amalgamation of the publishers businesses, they hoped to make economies of scale and savings in order to offer some relief from the slightly shrinking market. This also applies for information provisioning, which needed to become more uniform.

As part of this current phase of work, an extensive project will lead to the organization of a newspaper branch, a magazine branch, a branch for specialist publications and periodicals, and a considerably smaller branch for books and other media. A new branch, Electronic media will be set up completely outside the structure. This phase was set up two years ago: it will however run for one more year.

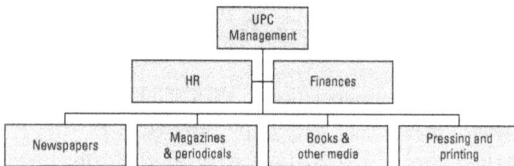

Figure 33 The UPC structure

Business information management

A start has also been made with the organization of business information management. There are a few reasons for this:

- Management of information provisioning: it is not known what, where, and why people pay money to IT.
- The second important argument is the re-structuring of the organization. As it is unclear who decides on information

provisioning and as every publisher has its own systems, there is a need for clarity and transparency of processes.

With this, an early beginning has been made on the standardization and centralization of business information management. This sometimes causes some problems: the centralization of information provisioning is running ahead of schedule compared with the processes and the user organization. This is indeed not according to the booklet but it also helps again in achieving the centralization of the business processes.

There are a number of objectives behind the restructuring and centralization of business information management:

- The first objective is a more businesslike control of the IT and information provisioning. This was characterized in the past by changes and investments being carried out without asking why this was done and sometimes with undesired effects.
- A second objective is that more resources are desired: business information management is carried out at several locations in the company and one is thus largely dependent on the work of a single person. More range and less dependence on people are required and re-use of existing knowledge is important.
- The third objective is that UPC desires more uniformity in information provisioning. Each part within UPC has its own interpretation and methods. Due to a higher level of uniformity, one expects lower costs but also more flexibility and more transparency. Figures throughout organization's departments are comparable. One must start with a uniform demand organization in order to achieve this uniformity in information provisioning. One would also expect this to lead to fewer discussions and tribal wars within the company.

- A final objective, but one which plays less of a role, is that it is easier to manage a central body than all the existing groups.

Structure

Within UPC, there is not one business information management (BIM) group but there are four organizations/groups dealing with the design of information provisioning.

There are three groups that also have tasks in the area of operational business information management. There is for example a group that carries out business information management for information provisioning related to the administrative processes surrounding the subscriptions (including the distribution) and the advertisements. This group is still in the newspaper department. The link between subscriptions and advertisements is quite loose.

Another BIM group deals with printing and setting. The automation of this group is more technical by nature and plays more of a role in the primary process of the publishers, i.e., preparing and printing.

There is also a group that deals with the support of the financial- and the personnel information provisioning.

Originally, there was also a policy group, CIM. This old information strategy department at the time did not go along with the privatization of VGK. This group maintains technology developments and makes policy in the area of information provisioning. In practice, this group acts quite independently of the other groups in the area of information provisioning. The links are therefore also poor.

The completion of business information management

An extensive start has been made on the centralization of business information management as a derivative of the centralization of the line organization as described. This centralization phase will last another one to one-and-a-half years. This still does not complete the centralization of business information management.

The group in which the business information management takes place for the subscription system works for the large departments in the company but a few smaller departments also still carry out business information management tasks themselves. The management towards the suppliers is also completely incumbent on this group. The centralization phase for business information management therefore regularly runs ahead on the centralization of the actual organization. The BIM group Subscriptions & Advertisements is placed within the newspaper branch but operates also for the other departments such as magazines. The newspaper department is by far the strongest organization within UPC and fulfils a pioneering role. This task is substantial by nature as the business is substantial by nature. This means BIM-Subscriptions & Advertisements is also the strongest BIM group. It is also clear that this will not remain so for ever: the group will finally be included as a staff department at company level.

Information provisioning

The BIM group Subscriptions & Advertisements provides information provisioning for the administrative processes supporting the subscriptions and advertisements.

The subscription administration is completely supported by the PARIS system. In this system, various data on subscribers

and subscriptions such as name and address details, types of
subscription, and other temporary addresses can be registered.
The distribution of the newspapers to the delivery points from
where they are distributed to the suppliers is also part of PARIS.
The entire financial handling of the subscriptions, invoicing,
and debtor administration, including the delivery costs, are also
included in PARIS. The system is one of VGK's most important
packages.

For the advertisements, UPC still has a few systems in use that
are in serious need of replacement. This legacy dates back to
the age of separate information provisioning with the various
publishers. Not one of the systems offers enough functionality
and possibilities to cover information provisioning for the entire
UPC, therefore a project is being started next year to select a new
system.

The Internet is also becoming more and more important for
information provisioning. The web applications are either linked
to the systems such as PARIS or are completely stand-alone and
deliver data to the systems via interface files.

VGK and UPC
VGK was originally the UPC IT department. It was privatized
five years ago and the shares are partly owned by large
external IT organizations. The PARIS package, for integrated
subscription administration for publishers is an important part of
VGK's services.

VGK has considerably increased its number of clients over the
past years with the result that the PARIS package is also used by

other publishers. UPC is however still the largest user of PARIS and still has a lot of influence.

As a result of the privatization, a start has been made to turn VGK into a more professional and business focused organization. VGK was forced by the clients and to a great extent by UPC to work in a more result-oriented and cheaper manner. ASL was adopted for this, which also affected UPC. This increased professionalism also made it necessary for UPC to approach the activities in a more structured manner.

ANNEX 2
BiSL and its environment

ASL and BiSL

Business information management is the term used to describe the activities of those people in a user organization who deal with the supporting and design of information provisioning. Business information management is carried out by people who state from the organizational perspective what the system should do, who support the end users, and ensure that information provisioning provides maximum support to the organization. The term application management was often used for these activities in the past. In the Looijen and Delen terminology (currently used as standard terms, see also chapter 1), the term application management is however used for the (technical) management and maintenance of applications and information systems. This includes activities such as programming, testing, designing and various other activities. ASL is the standard framework adopted for this.

ASL and BiSL have a joint source of development and therefore fit in with one another. ASL is for application management and IT organizations that develop and maintain information systems and applications. BiSL is for users and principals of IT. The ASL and BiSL profiles fit in with each other although there is no definite necessity for implementing and using ASL and BiSL at the same time.

ISPL and BiSL

ISPL (Information Systems Procurement Library) is a framework
that places the procurement (acquisition) of information
provisioning in a central role. It is based on defining the demand
and delivery of IT services. ISPL thus has a very large overlap
mainly with the business information management of information
provisioning (but also not completely). ISPL does not cover as
wide a range as BiSL and is mainly based on the procurement
of information provisioning. It does not therefore cover all of
business information management/information management (and
BiSL). ISPL on the other hand goes further than BiSL regarding
issues such as strategic supplier management and contract
management and is to be considered as a very valuable fulfillment
and addition of such processes.

ITIL and BiSL

ITIL is a framework developed by the British Government,
initially for its own use. It consists of a number of publications
in which an integrated process-like framework is described for
managing IT services through their life cycle. The best practices
that were described in the first versions of ITIL were mostly
derived from and applicable in the IT infrastructure domain.
Nowadays ITIL is positioned as a service management model for
all IT management domains.

ITIL refers to business information management within its
guidance and considers this within the scope of IT service
management itself. However, ITIL only describes activities
within business information management that are prerequisites
for fulfilling the role of IT service provider and focusses on the
activities of the service providers. BiSL describes a large range

of business information management activities, intended to be carried out within the user organization itself.

ITIL is known and used worldwide. It indirectly formed the starting point for the development of BiSL. Therefore there is a clear link between BiSL and ITIL.

Prince 2 and BiSL

Prince 2 is a project management method. It can be used within BiSL as a more project-oriented and more detailed method for managing projects that realize major changes to the information provisioning.

BiSL especially fits with the activities within the line organization. Prince 2 can be used in (large scale) renewal operations. The processes and activities of BiSL, especially those on the managing and operational levels, will to a large extent be a part of the project planning.

ANNEX 3
Promoting BiSL

BiSL is a public domain standard within a foundation. This foundation, the ASL BiSL Foundation, was established in 2002 by a number of like-minded organizations that place a great deal of emphasis on professionalism of application management and wish to promote this through the foundation. This takes place through publications, congresses, theme evenings, and collecting and publishing best practices in this area. The Board of Directors consists of representatives of the partners. In 2005 the promotion of BiSL was added to the foundation. The aim is to professionalize both supply and demand of IT services.

Objectives
The foundation's rationale is the joint working to improve and support the members in:
- Improving the management processes within the application management domain and the business information management domain.
- Sharing knowledge and information on ASL and BiSL.
- Developing and adopting best practices.
- Improving relations between the primary business processes and the IT function.

Activities

The foundation initiates the following activities:

– *Best practices*
  The participating parties offer best practices. The foundation
  evaluates the quality of these and makes these available to the
  public.

– *Metrics, sizing and tools*
  Making the quality and output of ASL and BiSL measurable
  is one of the objectives of the foundation. The quality of the
  execution of the processes can also be improved by developing
  tools that align well with the ASL and BiSL processes. The
  foundation also works on a sizing model to get insight into
  the necessary size of business information management
  organizations.

– *Education*
  The education of application managers, business information
  managers, information managers, the management, and
  the employees who ensure completion of the support
  of the business processes by IT is of great importance.
  The foundation ensures together with an independent
  examinations institute that valuable examinations can
  be taken. Training institutes can be accredited. Training
  institutes (for intermediate/higher vocational education and
  universities) are also encouraged to include ASL and BiSL in
  their curriculum.

– *Standardization*
  Together with the NEN (Nederlands Normalisatie-instituut)
  the foundation has set up standards for establishing maturity

levels of application management organizations. Service providers in application management can be assessed and certified by an independent institute. The foundation thus contributes to an increase in the quality of suppliers on offer.

– *Publicity*
Publicity is certainly crucial in the initial phase of a new open standard. The foundation arranges articles, presentations, books, congresses, and other media in order to bring ASL and BiSL to the attention of the respective target groups. All publications can be requested or ordered via the website and/or e-mail.

Participation

International participation is possible on three levels:

– *Individual membership*
Individual members can actively participate in the activities. They have access to the best practices, receive the newsletter and receive discounts on ASL and BiSL books and events.

– *International Partnership Silver*
All employees of an organization have the same rights as the individual participants. Silver International Partners have the right to use the ASL and BiSL logos for marketing purposes, have access to the best practices of participating organizations, receive the ASL BiSL Foundation newsmail and receive discounts on ASL and BiSL books and events. The partner is mentioned in presentations and on the website and a link to their own site is provided.

–   *International Partnership Gold*
    In addition to the rights of Silver International Partners, the
    Gold International Partners receive a discount of 10% on
    tariffs of ASL or BiSL gurus and receive local support from a
    representative of the ASL BiSL Foundation.

More information?

Click on www.aslbislfoundation.org or send a request to info@
aslbislfoundation.org.

ANNEX 4
More information

Literature

Van der Pols, Donatz, Van Outvorst, *BiSL - A Framework for Business Information Management* (second revised edition), Van Haren Publishing, 2012, 978 90 8753 702 9
This book (second edition) contains the description of the BiSL framework and serves as the main reference.

Backer, Van der Pols. *ASL, a management guide,* Van Haren Publishing 2003, 2006, ISBN 978 90 77212 84 4
The ASL framework is described here in analogue manner as in this Pocket Guide. The central case in this booklet is VGK, the most important supplier of the case in this book.

Van der Pols, *ASL2, a framework for Application Management,* Van Haren Publishing 2012, ISBN 978 90 8753 313 7
This book describes the latest version of the complete ASL framework.

Many more books, articles and white papers on BiSL have been written in Dutch. Some of the articles and white papers have been translated into English. Information can be found on the website of the ASL BiSL Foundation.

ASL BiSL Foundation

The ASL BiSL Foundation manages the body of thought
of ASL and BiSL. The website www.aslbislfoundation.org
provides information and best practices on ASL, BiSL, and the
foundation.

ANNEX 5
The complete BiSL framework

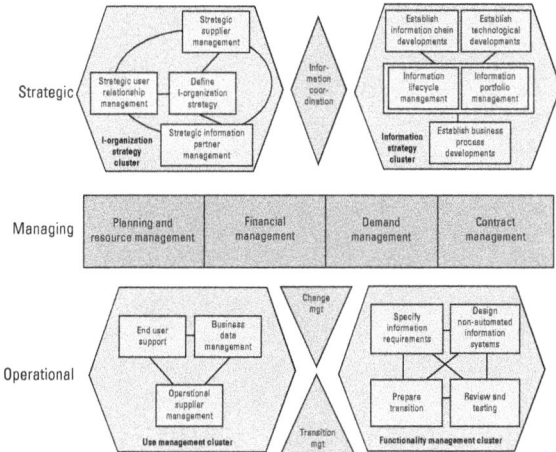

Strategic

- I-organization strategy cluster
  - Strategic supplier management
  - Strategic user relationship management
  - Define I-organization strategy
  - Strategic information partner management

- Information coordination

- Information strategy cluster
  - Establish information chain developments
  - Establish technological developments
  - Information lifecycle management
  - Information portfolio management
  - Establish business process developments

Managing

| Planning and resource management | Financial management | Demand management | Contract management |

Operational

- Use management cluster
  - End user support
  - Business data management
  - Operational supplier management

- Change mgt
- Transition mgt

- Functionality management cluster
  - Specify information requirements
  - Design non-automated information systems
  - Prepare transition
  - Review and testing

Index

www.ingramcontent.com/pod-product-compliance
Lightning Source LLC
Chambersburg PA
CBHW032330210326
41518CB00041B/2050